High Country Women
Pioneers of Yosemite National Park

Chris Enss

RIVERBEND
PUBLISHING

High Country Women: Pioneers of Yosemite National Park
© 2013 Chris Enss
Published by Riverbend Publishing, Helena, Montana

ISBN 13: 978-1-60639-068-9
Printed in the United States of America.

2 3 4 5 6 7 8 9 FS 25 24 23 22

Cover design by DD Dowden
Text design by Barbara Fifer

Front cover photo, left: Ta-bu-ce (Maggie Howard) COURTESY OF YOSEMITE NPS LIBRARY; front cover right: Beth Rodden making the first ascent of Meltdown, a 70-foot 5.14 crack at Upper Cascade Falls PHOTO © COREY RICH / AURORA PHOTOS; back cover: Clare Hodges COURTESY OF YOSEMITE NPS LIBRARY

Riverbend Publishing
P.O. Box 5833
Helena, MT 59604
riverbendpublishing.com

Contents

Acknowledgments

I am indebted to:

Linda Eades at the Yosemite Research Library at Yosemite National Park.

Barbara Puorro Galasso, photographer at the George Eastman House, International Museum of Photography and Film.

Sara Hay, Museum Technician at Eugene O'Neill National Historic Site.

Erin Davenport, Compliance Specialist at Yosemite National Park.

Kristin Olsen, Assemblymember, 25th Assembly District, California.

Beth Rodden, award-winning rock climber.

And most especially Kathleen Correia, Supervising Librarian, California History Section at the California State Library.

Foreword
by
California Assemblymember Kristin Olsen

When I was a girl growing up in California's San Joaquin Valley, my family regularly sought refuge from the Central Valley's dry, hot summers in the neighboring picturesque Sierra Nevada mountain range. As we traveled to Yosemite and surrounding areas, I can remember staring out the window, amazed at the incredible scenery complete with infinitely tall redwood trees and impossibly large mountains of rock. I remember breathing in the clean mountain air as we exited the car, and the exhilaration I felt upon seeing the thunderous waterfalls along the Vernal Falls trail, while water sprinkled my face. And just like that, all of life's worries were replaced with playful laughter and the tranquility that only the Yosemite area can provide.

Years later, I was honored to represent the Yosemite area as a member of the California State Assembly. I worked hard to make sure other, more urban areas of the state understood the value and importance of the Sierra Nevada, and I advocated for the people who live there and the rich natural resources the area encompasses.

When I had the opportunity to read *High County Women: Pioneers of Yosemite National Park*, it was as if I found a whole new appreciation for the place I feel I've known my entire life. Places I had visited time and time again suddenly took on new life as I understood the hard work and dedication that the women profiled in this book readily invested to make Yosemite a place that we can all enjoy.

Chris Enss not only does a noteworthy job of documenting history for us, but she breathes life back into the women who were so integral to the shaping and preservation of the greater Yosemite area. You come to understand through Ms. Enss' work that Mrs. Louisa Stentzel Muir's gentle and unselfish nature encouraged her husband, John Muir, to make several treks in the western United States, leaving herself and their two daughters at home for several months at a time. And you feel the sense of pride that Clare Hodges must have felt when she was appointed the nation's only female park ranger during World War I.

While the women profiled in this book are by no means the only females whose lives directly and indirectly influenced Yosemite, the book is a great tribute to those who selflessly worked to document and protect the area for the benefit of posterity and future generations. We must continue to work toward the promotion and preservation of Yosemite with the same level of dedication and commitment that those in these pages exhibited.

If you've never had the chance to experience the breathtaking beauty of Yosemite Valley, there is no question you are missing out. Plan an adventure that will take you there to experience the wonders of its awe-inspiring landscape. Even if you've been there time and time again as I have, I implore you to read about the women in this book. I'm confident that you, like me, will develop a deeper appreciation for the hard work contributed by these women who gave us the opportunity to revel in Yosemite's magnificence and beauty.

Introduction

The United States was preoccupied with a Civil War when Congress approved the measure and President Abraham Lincoln signed it, that made Yosemite a national park. In spite of the terrible strife the country was experiencing, politicians and conservationists believed action needed to be taken to preserve this wilderness nestled in the Sierra Nevada mountains.[1]

The 761,000 acres that featured giant sequoia groves with trees thousands of years old, and many unique geological formations, had been the destination of choice for many fur trappers and adventurers. In the mid-1820s, beaver, bear, and mountain lion hides were in great demand, and expanding the nation's boundaries beyond the Mississippi River was encouraged by entrepreneurs and officeholders. Fearful that Yosemite's natural beauty would be eroded away by the progress of civilization, concerned individuals pressed lawmakers to make the area off limits to gold-seekers, hunters, and land developers. On June 30, 1864, Yosemite became the first scenic reservation created by a central government.[2]

Frontiersman Joseph Reddeford Walker is credited with discovering Yosemite Valley in 1833 when he led an expedition of fifty men into the mountainous California territory. In 1849 a sea of humanity began migrating west after the Sacramento-area gold strike. Driven by the Gold Rush and a desire to settle in a new land, prospectors, farmers, businessmen, ranchers, inn keepers, cooks, laundresses, teachers, and entertainers hurried to the West Coast. Men and women miners and their families, with the intention of stripping the region of its gold, pushed their way past the Native Americans living in the Yosemite Valley. Indians who resisted the incursion of small gold mining operations on the Merced River were moved to a reservation near Fresno.[3]

White men such as naturalist John Muir and women such as author and political activist Jessie Fremont opposed the idea of mining in the scenic locale. Both believed the natural beauty of the area and wildlife would be threatened if exposed to toxic chemicals used to separate gold ore from rock. John had spent years studying Yosemite Valley's geology and botany and had determined its mountain ranges were formed by glacial erosion. The Maidu, Miwok, and Paiute Indians disagreed with his research. Indian legend passed down from father to son and mother to daughter holds that the mountain Half Dome, her husband, Washington Tower, and their infant son did it all.[4]

As the story goes, Half Dome lived with her husband, Washington Tower, on the bank of the Merced River at a point on the edge of the San Joaquin Valley. Owing to some quarrel with her husband, Half Dome ran away toward the east. As she proceeded up through the mountains she created the upper course of the Merced River and the Yosemite Valley itself. She carried a burden basket, a finely feathered basket, and her baby in its cradle. In the finely feathered basket she carried a smaller basket containing seeds of various kinds which she planted all along the way. Hence, there are many different kinds of these trees and foods now.

Finding that his wife had left him, Washington Tower cut a white oak club and started after her. He overtook her near the point where this great peak now stands. She had taken her baby out of its cradle basket and placed it on the top of the load in the burden basket, carrying the cradle meanwhile under her arm.

Washington Tower whipped Half Dome severely. The burden basket was broken and fell with its contents into Mirror Lake. It has never since been seen. The basket containing the seeds was thrown to the north side of the canyon. It landed bottom up and became North Dome.

Half Dome threw the baby cradle against the north wall of the canyon where it now appears in the Royal Arches.

As Half Dome received her punishment, she wept bitterly and was transformed into the great peak. The dark colored streaks on the vertical wall on the north of Half Dome are the tear stains on her face. She wore, at the time, a buckskin dress, but nothing now remains to indicate it.

The club Washington Tower used was finally thrown aside. It landed upright in the center of Mirror Lake and remained there for some time as a large, black snag. When Washington Tower had spent his wrath he went over to the north side of the valley where he has since remained—a great shaft of granite.

Maria Lebrado, a member of the original Yosemite Indian tribe, shared this tale about the origin of the region with the pioneers who moved into the valley, the majority of which were men. Only ten percent of the white population that invaded Yosemite in the early 1850s were women. Though their numbers were few, the impact they had on the areas was as lasting as the exploits of Half Dome. For example, Elvira Hutchings came to Yosemite with her husband in 1855 and began her career as one of the original inn keepers in the valley. She was more than twenty years younger than her husband, James Mason Hutchings, the man who led the first tour party into Yosemite. Their marriage didn't last but the inn she helped establish did.[5]

Ida Tinsley Howard was the valley's first schoolmarm in 1876. She came west with her father, who operated a resort on Mirror Lake at the east end of Yosemite. Ida made sure her students were proficient in math, especially algebra.[6]

Carefree maid and waitress Kitty Tatch was a pioneer in the field of photography in Yosemite, in front of the camera, however, not behind. She was unafraid of heights and posed precariously on ledges and cliffs around the park. Pictures of her were sold as postcards to visitor at valley restaurants and stage stops.[9]

In 1905, Agnes Wikenson, Ann Taurer, Ethel and Ann Fullerton were the first women in Yosemite to be held up by a highwayman. The stagecoach the ladies were traveling in was stopped by an armed, masked bandit who took all the money the women had. The stage passengers continued on to their destination, a campsite near Indian Village, and were in the valley when the fugitive was arrested by authorities in Sacramento two days after the incident.[10]

High Country Women: Pioneers of Yosemite National Park focuses on the tough-fibered individuals like the aforementioned ladies who caught the virulent Western fever that led them to the spot known as the crown jewel of American's National Parks.

I chose ten women to profile in this book—all, truly so invincible spirits. As that they worthily represent the sturdy character of women who made their home in one of the most famous, breathtakingly beautiful spots in America.

Jessie Fremont

Guardian of Yosemite

Jessie Fremont, an attractive, modestly dressed, very pregnant eighteen-year-old with dark eyes and an inviting smile, sat at a desk in a cozy room in a Washington, D.C., home, feverishly writing. Her husband, the twenty-nine-year-old celebrated explorer and politician, John Fremont, sat across from her on a massive leather chair, describing in detail the 1842 expedition over the Rocky Mountains into Oregon in which he participated. Jessie jotted down every aspect of the experience John relayed to her. Where details were lacking, she encouraged her spouse to elaborate about what he saw, how the great uncharted area looked and smelled, and what the inhabitants, if any, of the land were like.[1]

For more than a month the couple had made a point to discuss the journeys in which John had embarked. Early every morning they would sequester themselves in their home's study, and John would relive his experiences. Jessie translated her spouse's adventures onto paper for curious, westward-moving settlers.[2] According to John's memoirs, Jessie had a talent for visualizing the trips he had taken and writing what she saw. Her intelligence, perception, and devotion made her an ideal collaborator. The Fremonts combined forces to create numerous publications used to aid miners, soldiers, and government surveyors in their quest to conquer the West and revel in such beautiful locales as Bear Valley and Yosemite.[3]

Jessie Ann Benton Fremont, the woman historians referred to as the "guardian of Yosemite," was born on May 31, 1824, in the Blue Ridge Mountains of Virginia. Her father, Thomas Hart Benton, was an ambitious man who went from farming into politics and eventually became a United States senator from Missouri (and great-uncle of 20th-century muralist Thomas Hart Benton). Jessie visited Washington, D.C., often as a child, and met with such luminaries as President Andrew Jackson and Congressman Davy Crockett.[4]

Jessie and her sister, Elizabeth, attended the capital's leading girl's boarding school, alongside the daughters of other political leaders and wealthy business owners. It was for that very reason Jessie disliked school. "There was no end to the conceit, the assumption, the class distinction there," she wrote in her memoirs. In addition to the lines drawn between the children of various social standings, Jessie felt the studies were not challenging to her. "I was miserable in the narrow, elitist atmosphere. I learned nothing there," she recalled in her journal. The best thing about attending school was the opportunity it afforded her to meet John Fremont, the man who would become her husband.[5]

Born on January 21, 1813, John was an intelligent, attractive man with gray-blue eyes who excelled in mathematics and craved adventure. While awaiting an assignment from the United States Corp of Topographical Engineers [a war department agency engaged in exploring and mapping unknown regions of the United States], John was introduced to Thomas Benton. Benton was a key proponent in Washington for western expeditions. He and John discussed the great need for the land west of the Missouri River to be explored. Benton invited the young surveyor and map maker to continue the conversation at his home over a meal with his family. It there that Jessie and John first met, and they were instantly smitten with each other. Within a year, they were wed.[6]

Jessie Benton was sixteen years old, and John Fremont was twenty-seven when they married on October 19, 1841. The newlyweds lived at the

Jessie Fremont—American writer, political activist, and protector of Yosemite.

Gatsby Hotel on Capitol Hill until John was assigned to lead a four-month expedition to the Rocky Mountains. Jessie helped him prepare for the journey by reviewing information about the plant life, Indian encampments, and rock formations he would come in contact with during his trip. John headed west on May 2, 1842. Jessie, who was pregnant with their first child, moved into a small apartment near her parents' home.[7]

John returned to Washington, D.C., in November 1842, just two weeks before their daughter was born. He watched over baby Elizabeth Benton "Lily" Fremont while Jessie reviewed the slim notes John had taken during the expedition and fashioned a report for the government using his data and detailed recollections of life on the trail. Politicians such as Missouri Senator Lewis Linn praised the report for being not only practical and informative but entertaining as well. The material would be used by emigrants as a guidebook.[8]

The report read like an adventure while providing pertinent instructions for travel over the Great Plains, including the best locations for hunting, grazing spots for livestock, and obtaining water. Portions of the report were reprinted in newspapers throughout the East Coast and the enthusiastic response for his efforts brought John instant notoriety. Jessie was elated for her husband and thrilled by the encouragement she received for her contribution. Becoming a full time author was now her life's pursuit.[9]

In early 1843, John moved his family to St. Louis, Missouri, where his next expedition would be originating. Jessie took on the role as John's secretary, reviewing mail from suppliers and frontiersmen such as Kit Carson. She wrote the necessary correspondence to members of the Topographical Bureau, updating them on the progress and the date the expedition would begin, how long it would take, and what they planned to accomplish. Shortly before John departed to explore a route to the Pacific Coast, a letter came to the Fremonts' home instructing him to postpone the expedition until questions over a request to purchase weapons had been settled. Fearing the entire mission would be jeopardized if the journey was delayed, Jessie did not give the letter to her husband. John set out on the expedition on May 13, 1843. He returned home the following August, having successfully begun opening up the great territory between the Mississippi Valley and California.[10]

Jessie again translated the notes and stories about John's venture into a captivating narrative. The report was widely circulated, and prompted numerous people to move to California and Oregon seeking a better life.

The government approved third expedition over the Rocky Mountains. Between May 1845 and 1849, John would trek back and forth from his home with Jessie and his daughter to the Pacific Coast two more times. He uncovered new and better routes to an area many pioneers referred to as a "veritable paradise."[11]

In May 1849, Jessie and her daughter traveled to San Francisco to join John already in California. The seaport town was crowded with people who had heard rumors that there was gold in the hills around Sacramento. John wasn't interested in prospecting. But because lumber was in great demand, he decided to invest in a saw mill. The investment proved to be a wise one. The mill made a substantial profit in a short amount of time. John used a portion of his earnings to purchase a large ranch near Yosemite Valley. Jessie described the area where her new home was located, and the spectacular Sierra Nevada Mountain Range in glowing terms in her memoirs:

> The new day brought us into an enchanting natural park
> of grassy uplands and fir and hemlock growths in varying
> stages. The layered boughs, tipped with the lighter green of
> the spring growth, rested in tent-like spread on soft young
> grass and wildflowers. It was all gracious and open and smil-
> ing with, at times, a break in the trees giving us a glimpse
> across the valley below of the near Yosemite range.[12]

It wasn't until the cold weather had passed through the Sierras completely that the Fremonts spent any extended period of time in Yosemite. Jesse struggled with bad health en route to California, and her lungs were frail. She needed to be in a warm spot until she was better. John found a home in Monterey where they stayed for several weeks. In the summer of 1849, the Fremonts relocated to a cottage in Bear Valley, west of Yosemite. The grandeur of the setting moved Jesse so that she filled pages in her journal with thoughts about the experience.

> This lovely valley is rimmed about by ranges of moun-
> tains rising from green foothills to the dark Sierra, snow-
> crowned,.Its glittering summits made the culminating touch

of beauty—and the defense for us—"so far, but no farther," its snow-peaks said. Even the trees were in color. They have feathery fern-like foliage of tender white-green with long clusters of berries, the size and clear color of red currants.[13]

In addition to writing about Yosemite's extraordinary scenery, Jessie also wrote about its dangers. While horseback riding one day with John and her children, Jessie heard what she thought was a dog barking. It didn't take John long to recognize the sound was really a bear. Without saying a word, he grabbed the reins of the horse Jessie was riding, turned the animal around, and quickly led it away from the bark.

It was no dog, but a grizzly bear that made that warning bark, and we were very close to it, [she remembered in her journal]. My ignorance spared me the shock of this knowledge…it was not only a bear, but a she-bear with cubs. John knew she would not be likely to leave her cubs unless we came nearer or irritated her by talking and making noises. Horses are terribly afraid of this powerful and dangerous animal, and one danger was that our horses would break away and run for safety leaving us to the chances of getting off on foot. There I was the weak link in the chain. My daughter was fleet of foot and so steady of nerve that she was told the truth at once, and did her part bravely in keeping me unaware of any unusual condition.[14]

The Fremonts' initial time at the Bear Valley cottage was short lived. Jessie's health took a turn and the family returned to Monterey as soon as they could. John needed to do so not only for his wife's sake but also for California's. He was being encouraged by Washington politicians to help create a civilian territorial government and to lead the way to statehood. In December 1849, John was named the Democratic candidate for the United States Senate. The following year he was sworn in to the post. Jessie proved to be a capable politician's wife. She hosted delegate meetings and spoke out against slavery and why California should be admitted to the Union as a free state. Jessie's influence and John's perseverance played major roles in bringing about that outcome. On December 9, 1850, California became the thirty-first state.[15]

On April 19, 1851, Jessie gave birth to their second child, John Charles. By the time John was two and his sister was nine, they had already traveled with their parents to New York, Europe, and Africa. Prior to returning to California Jessie had another child, a girl. Anne Beverly was born on February 1, 1853. John did not stay around long after Ann arrived. Congress had approved several still-confidential routes between the thirty-second and forty-seventh parallels. John helped map out a passage for the Pacific Railroad to travel.[16]

After John's two failed attempts to run for the office of President of the United States and embarking in several more survey missions, the Fremonts returned to their home near Yosemite in 1858. They had been gone so long their Bear Valley home was in a state of disrepair. Jessie worked hard to transform the rugged, two-story house into an aesthetically pleasing cottage. In addition to adding French wallpaper and Chinese silk curtains to the interior, she had the outside white-washed. The family referred to the home as the "White House." "It was all peaceful and beautiful beyond telling," Jessie wrote in her memoirs about the White House and the views from every window.

> The grand beauty of the Yosemite country, lying just
> across from us like a great panorama in a vast amphitheater,
> was of endless attraction. Sunrise and sunset made marvels
> of color and varying effects, and the still blaze of golden
> noon had its own splendid charm.[17]

Horace Greely, the famous political activist and editor of the *New York Tribune*, visited the Fremonts at their Bear Valley home in the spring of 1859. It was Horace's first trip to the far west, and, he, like many other well-known individuals who saw Yosemite, was just as captivated by the spectacular setting as Jessie. Jessie shared with Horace that her time in Bear Valley had been "better than all the days of my life." It was her description of Yosemite and the time spent living there that helped persuade Congress to set aside thousands of acres of the Yosemite Valley and the neighboring Mariposa Grove of big trees (now officially the Mariposa Grove of Giant Sequoias) to someday be used as a state park.[18]

In 1864 Jessie called together several influential people who had visited her and her family during their time in Yosemite, including Greely, minister and politician Thomas Starr King; U.S. Senator Edward Baker of Oregon; a representative for the Central American Steam Transit Company, Israel Ward Raymond; and journalist and landscape designer Frederick Law Olmsted, to compile photographs, sketches, and research material of the area to be presented to President Abraham Lincoln. She hoped the information would help persuade the president to protect the picturesque valley from mining and lumber companies who wanted to take over the land. Some of the natural marvels Jessie and the cohort of people she enlisted were Half Dome, a stone mountain on the eastern side of Yosemite; El Capitan, a smooth slab of rocks more than thirty-six-hundred feet high that stands guard near the valley entrance; and the lovely, wispy, wind-blown Bridalveil Falls.[19] Israel Raymond drafted the letter that explained in detail the vital need to protect the wonders of Yosemite. On June 30, 1864, President Lincoln signed a bill that made certain Yosemite would be held "for public use, resort, and recreation for all time."[20]

Jessie was pleased with the decision the president had made and noted in her memoirs the importance preserving the section of California would have on generations to come.

> Children who have the disadvantage of only town life,
> or the opera bouffe [comic opera] life of "summer resorts"
> known nothing of the many and progressive delights of
> country children. To the town boy an apple is represented
> by pennies and a fruit stand. He knows nothing of the ed-
> ucation in weather, in patience, in observation of the many
> phases that lead from the icicled tree to its rosy blossoms,
> and the little green knobs he eyes without fingering, on [to]
> the full-ripened fruit, which has for him a bouquet of mean-
> ing and flavor and triumph money cannot buy.

It was Jessie's sincere belief that children, as well as adults, who visited Yosemite would be able to learn a great deal from the land.[21]

While Jessie fought to save the glacier-carved valley of Yosemite, John fought in the Union Army during the Civil War. President Lincoln made him a major general in charge of the Department of the West. Fremont's military accomplishments were beyond reproach. At the conclusion of the war John devoted himself to the promotion of a southern railroad across the continent, spending a great deal of his time with his wife and children in France soliciting funds for the venture.[22]

From 1878 to 1881, Jessie and John lived in Prescott, Arizona, while John served as governor of the territory. Jessie helped support the family by writing stories for various magazines, including a publication for children entitled *Wide Awake*. In 1890 the book she penned about life in California, specifically her time in the Yosemite Valley, was published. *Far-West Sketches* was a popular seller among travelers to the Sierra Foothills. That same year, John died suddenly of peritonitis.[23]

Jessie was heartbroken by her husband's death. "Like a bolt came from the clear sky the blow fell," she later wrote in her memoirs about John's demise. Newspapers such as the June 5, 1890, edition of the *Piqua Daily Leader* in Piqua, Ohio, called John Fremont "America's Pathfinder" and credited him with doing more to open the vast American West "than any other man in United States history."

Jessie returned to California from New York, where she and John had been living at the time of his death. She dealt with the grief of losing John by completing several of his unfinished writings. Those articles were later published in *Century Magazine*.[24]

Yosemite officially became a national park on October 1, in that sad year, showing Jessie some fruits from her efforts. In 1906 the surrounding area of Mariposa Grove was made part of the park as well.[25]

Jessie Ann Benton Fremont passed away on December 27, 1902, after a bout with pneumonia. She was seventy-eight years old. According to the December 29, 1902, edition of the *Fort Wayne Evening Sentinel*,

Mrs. Fremont was a remarkable woman, to whom the territory west of the Mississippi River owes more than to any other person perhaps in the country. She helped bring about the preservation of more than twelve-hundred square miles of land in Northern California known as Yosemite. She wielded an influence second to but few statesman of her generation.

Annie Ripley, Elizabeth Fry, Sara Haight, & Evelyn Bovial

Weddings and Honeymoons

A t the turn of the 20th century, Yosemite Valley, in particular the area known as Bridalveil Falls, was referred to as the "show place of the Sierras." Artists from every medium thought the falls cascading down more than six hundred feet of rock wall into the valley to be so beautiful that it was considered selfish for anyone who looked on the splendor of the setting not to share the pleasure with others using whatever talent they were given. Among the many famous guests who visited Yosemite National Park's prominent waterfall in the Yosemite Valley were General Ulysses S. Grant, Horace Greely, General William T. Sherman, and Ralph Waldo Emerson. Naturalist John Muir entreated the public to visit the spot often. According to his memoirs he challenged park patrons to "climb the mountains and get their good tidings." He assured them that "nature's peace will flow into you as sunshine into trees."[1]

It's not unusual that many couples chose the stunning Bridalveil Falls as the backdrop for their nuptials. The first bride to plan her wedding at the spot was a prominent young woman from Los Angeles. According to the August 6, 1901, edition of the *Boston Globe*, the ceremony was "so incredible it defied description and started a trend in civil unions held at the majestic National Park." The stunning setting would be duplicated by hundreds of betrothed couples in the early 1900s.

With a mighty altar and the generous diapason of an incomparable waterfall furnishing the melody of a bridal march Miss Annie Ripley of Los Angeles and Henry C. Best of San Francisco were wed in the valley a few days ago [the *Globe* continued]. It was the first marriage ceremony performed in Yosemite, and for solemnity and picturesqueness it was surpassingly notable."[2]

One hundred guests were present and walked with the bride and groom over trails and under trees to where the water crashed upon rocks beneath towering cliffs on either side. The *Globe* continued,

> The day was a superb one and the scene one of matchless beauty.
>
> Miss Ripley was prettily attired in a mountain costume and the man who was to be made her husband had set aside the customary garments and wore camping attire as well. Their look was fitting for the setting.
>
> The Yosemite

Historical photograph of Bridalveil Falls.
COURTESY OF THE CALIFORNIA HISTORY ROOM, CALIFORNIA STATE LIBRARY, SACRAMENTO, CALIFORNIA

populace made a holiday of it all. Men and women were brilliantly dressed and formed an attractive group when they arrived at the base of the falls a half an hour before noon. The Bohemian string orchestra was in attendance and rendered exquisite melody from a natural choir loft on a gigantic rock.

As the prospective bride and groom walked toward the altar-like stone on which the ceremony was to take place the orchestra began the melodious wedding march. The music of the stringed instruments at times was lost in the roar of the falling water, and the efforts of the well-intentioned melody makers were almost futile in comparison with the strength of the storm of sound nature had provided.

At the rock altar stood Rev. Walter Freeman of Portland, Maine, who was a guest at the hotel in the valley. The bridal couple passed through the semi-circle of friends and took their position before the clergyman. Miss Ripley was accompanied by Miss Helen Ripley, the bridesmaid, and Mr. Durrell attended the groom. The words of the marriage ritual were spoken, and Mr. and Mrs. Best returned to receive congratulations from friends, family, and witnesses.

The entire party then proceeded to the hotel where an elaborate wedding breakfast was served. Late in the afternoon Mr. and Mrs. Best left the valley in a stage profusely decorated with white ribbons. They would spend their honeymoon among the giant sequoias of the Mariposa big tree grove.

Henry C. Best was a well-spoken artist, and was formerly employed by newspapers in San Francisco. He had come to Yosemite three months prior to paint scenery in the valley. He was a director of the Press Club in San Francisco.

The scenic wedding of Annie Ripley and Henry Best was the first recorded ceremony performed at Yosemite, but William Chapman

Ralston and his bride Elizabeth Fry were among the first to honeymoon at the park. The wedding journey from the Ralstons' villa in San Mateo County to Yosemite was written about quite extensively by wedding guests and Bay area newspapers.[5]

On May 20, 1858, William Ralston, a banker, business owner, and investor in the Comstock mine, and debutante Elizabeth "Lizzie" Fry were married in San Francisco. He was thirty-two and Lizzie was twenty-one. According to the September 30, 1888, edition of the *San Francisco Examiner*, the afternoon wedding was held at the Calvary Church on Bush Street:

> The church was crowded with their friends, and the bride,
> a pretty brunette looked charming in a most becoming
> wedding costume. A short reception followed at the home
> of Mrs. Darling at North Beach, and then the ladies of
> the party donned Bloomer dresses and all departed for a
> honeymoon camping-out frolic in the Yosemite Valley.

Sarah Haight, a member of the bride's party, was among the guests to accompany the newlyweds to the park. She recorded in her published journal that

> three steamers, the *Helen Hesley*, the *Sierra Nevada*, and
> the *Orizaba*, carrying selected family and friends left the
> wharf at four o'clock in the afternoon. As the boats pulled
> away from the harbor, hearty cheers were offered up to the
> happy couple and a salute was fired from the *Sierra Nevada*
> and the *Orizaba*. After traveling five days, first by steamer
> and then donkey, the wedding party passed through a cave
> which deposited the sojourners at the mouth of a cave which
> spilled out onto the Yosemite Valley. Looking up at the rock
> the stone formation around resembled a theatre with its side
> scenes. There were grotesque faces and bats and owls carved
> in rock, but when you change your position the resemblance
> would vanish.[4]

Sarah described the wildlife in the area, listing a variety of birds, lizards, and fish. There were obstacles along the path that impeded their

progress in some spots, like little mountain brooks to cross; pine trees had fallen; ferocious winds had covered crude trails with limbs and leaves. At one point, Sarah, along with the bride and groom and other guests, tried to walk the steep ascent to the top of a mountain. After two miles members of her party were too tired to go on and boarded their donkeys again. In the evenings the group slept in tents that had been erected for them, and dined on meals pre-

A happy couple exchanges vows at a romantic setting near Bridalveil Falls in a sketch dating from the 1890s.

pared over a campfire. "No supper that I ever ate tasted half so good as that one, the long ride having given us very good appetites," Sarah wrote in her journal.

On the morning of May 25, 1858, after five days on the trail, William Ralston, his new wife, Sarah, and the other guests arrived at the foot of the mountains. Sarah remembered that it was one of the "most magnificent prospects" she had ever beheld.

> The summits were so beautiful, green level prairie with a little stream flowing through its midst and the trees were all like orchard trees. So cultivated did it look that we could scarcely believe that it was not cultivated. Above it on the opposite side toward a mountain covered with pine trees, and still beyond that rose another and another, range on

range, and the last were covered with snow. How grateful the cold wind coming from the snow felt in the noon, and the snow was so pure and white that you could scarce distinguish it from the clouds resting midday on their sides. …Looking back of us we could see the coast range of mountains at a distance of two hundred miles and conspicuous among them was Mount Diablo. How that glimpse of the old veteran carried me home to my own room, where it is the first thing I can see on looking out of my window in the morning.

The road had been getting gradually wilder and the hills sterner. Immense granite rocks rest on the mountain above the trail with a threatening aspect. In some places they appear to have fallen and carried large pine trees along with them. In one place I saw where a large pine tree had torn up a rock in its fall, exactly as a dentist extracts a tooth with his pincers. This afternoon, when about two miles from the entrance of the valley, we saw the Bridalveil, the first fall in the valley. It looked like a silver thread in the distance and relieved the solemn grandeur of the surrounding hills.

After a short stop to enjoy the scenery, the wedding party continued onward.

We rode through beautiful green meadows, under the shady branches of trees, and the fragrance of the wild honeysuckle was a pleasant exchange for the reflection of the sun's rays from the great white rocks. We rode through beautiful green meadows, under the shady branches of trees, and the fragrance of the wild honeysuckle was a pleasant exchange for the reflection of the sun's rays from the great white rocks. To the right of us was what is called a "Cathedral" in the gothic style, and where could there be a church more magnificent? We rode on, at our left "El Capitan," a man wrapped in a Spanish cloak with a slouched

hat. We drew rein on the banks of the Merced, where it was very still and deep, and lay down on our blankets under the protection of the "sentinel." Never did the beauty of the Twenty-Third Psalm present itself so before me. I had been frightened and disturbed and was very weary, and the words, "He maketh me to lie down in green pastures; he leadeth me beside the still waters. — Yea, though I walk through the valley of the shadow of death, I will fear no evil; for thou art with me; thy rod and thy staff they comfort me," filled me with quiet and peace. We had been walking through the valley of the shadow of death, as it seemed. By my request the camp was called "Stillwater Camp."

From the camp we were not in sight of either of the falls, though we could hear very plainly. A large fire was burning.

All the party was tired and stretched themselves out in various postures, but I was so happy and so occupied with the beautiful scene that I could not sleep. Behind me was the Sentinel—it was only by lying on my back that I could see its summit 4,000 feet above me. The valley was in shade when the mood began to shine on the Sentinel's great bald head. I watched the moonlight creeping softly downwards until it was about half-way down its sides, and then I saw the moon itself advance hesitatingly above the brow of the opposite rocks. The [word missing in original] hesitated advance withdrew and then came boldly forward. She was closely followed by a star that advanced trembling to the edge of the rocks, rose and fell several times, then followed her mistress. Gradually the moonlight advanced and covered the whole camp and shone on the beautiful river.

Not long after the deluxe wagon train honeymoon, the Ralstons moved into a mansion William built for Elizabeth in San Mateo.[5]

In August 1915, newlyweds Seth and Evelyn Bovial traveled from Janesville, Wisconsin, to celebrate their union with a honeymoon in Yosemite National Park. Evelyn was completely taken with Yosemite. She spent evenings writing about the day's treks. Seth complained that his new wife was neglecting him. Married on August 28, 1915, in Milwaukee, Seth had hoped Evelyn's focus would be solely on him. "Some things are too beautiful not to write about," she recalled in her journal, "the trip must be noted for posterity's sake if nothing else."

Soon after, Evelyn submitted a detailed account of her venture to the September 9, 1915, edition of her hometown newspaper, the *Janesville Daily Gazette*, and Seth filed a petition to the court to have the marriage annulled. He was convinced the lack of attention Evelyn paid him was indicative of how she would treat him in the future. Thus, Evelyn Bovial was the first woman to have lost a husband for recording the extraordinary sights of Yosemite.[6]

Elizabeth Pershing

Adventurous Journalist

Twenty-four-year-old Lizzie K. Pershing stood at the base of Yosemite's South Dome (now called Half Dome) staring up at the mountain. A cold, stiff wind traveled across the rock with such force she struggled to keep her balance. She pulled her coat tightly around her shoulders and rubbed her gloved hand over the smooth stone. It was October 8, 1876, and Lizzie was still pondering the climb up the precipice, which was considered at the time to be the largest and highest in the world.[1]

Standing at the fork of the upper valley, South Dome is a solid, rocky loaf reaching six thousand feet above the ground. To Lizzie it appeared as though a powerful hand cut away the eastern half of the mountain, leaving a sheer cliff over a mile in height. According to the July 24, 1860, edition of the Milwaukee, Wisconsin, newspaper *The Daily Sentinel*, the first person to climb South Dome was a Scottish sailor and blacksmith named George Anderson of Montrose, and he did so in 1859. George was a skilled outdoorsman who later built a house near the saddle of the dome. During the summer of 1876 he began the difficult task of constructing a staircase of a thousand steps up the dome. He had hoped to have an elevator running by the start of fall in 1876 as well as a steam car that would carry passengers up the almost perpendicular walls. His dream was never realized.[2]

For his first climbing attempts, George collected turpentine from nearby pine trees and smeared his hands and feet with it. He put coarse bagging upon his extremities and covered it with pitch. After having several serious falls, one of them nearly fatal, he acknowledged the impracticality of all such methods, and tried the only one by which a mortal could ever accomplish this feat. Climbing as far as possible he drilled a hole in the rock. A wooden block was placed in this, and into it an iron pin was driven. Throwing a rope over this, he drew himself up and stood upon one pin while preparing a place in the rock for another, and so on to the top, which he reached at 4 p.m., October 12, 1875, two days and a half from when the first iron pin was placed in the rock.

"[George] Anderson began with Conway's old rope," John—a Yosemite Valley resident who also attempted to climb South Dome until he found it too hard and dangerous—wrote in his book *Treasures of Yosemite*. The rope "had been left in place, and [Anderson] resolutely drilled his way to the top, inserting eye-bolts five or six feet apart, and fastening his rope fast to each in succession, resting his feet on the last bolt while he drilled a hole for the next above. Occasionally, some irregularity in the curve, or slight foothold, would enable him to climb a few feet without the rope, which he would pass and begin drilling again...."[3] Since George first tackled the ascent to the top of South Dome, Lizzie and other visitors had gazed in wonder at the spikes driven into the rock and the hardy spirits who had repeatedly endeavored to scale it. The shreds of rope dangling in the wind told the story of their failure. Bighorn sheep had been spotted browsing on the hitherto-inaccessible peak. How they got there was a mystery. "They had plenty of grass to eat," Lizzie contemplated in her memoirs, "but no water, only the dew that fell on the dome at night."[4]

Lizzie made the South Dome climb using gear comprising ropes, harnesses, steel hooks, sturdy boots, and gloves. She carefully studied the method George used to attack the climb. She also read notes by naturalist John Muir about George's trek. Prior to George's 1859 climb most Yosemite explorers such as Josiah Whitney insisted the mountain would "never be trod by human foot."[5]

Lizzie had an overwhelming desire to conquer the mountain and share the journey to the top with interested readers curious about the western landscape. Born on April 4, 1852, in Pittsburgh, Pennsylvania, Elizabeth "Lizzie" Kate Pershing grew up listening to stories about the pioneers who ventured over the plains to settle in wild, remote territories. Her father, Reverend Israel C. Pershing (president of the Pittsburgh Female College) and her mother Charlotte Lucretia Canan

Half Dome, once known as South Dome.

encouraged their daughter's interest in the uncharted land and cheered her on when she decided to become a journalist and write about her adventures in the new land. At the time she was planning to ascend South Dome she was working as a correspondent for the *Pittsburgh Gazette* and the *Pittsburgh Telegraph* newspapers.[6]

Lizzie, who also went by the nickname "Percy," was described in glowing terms by friends and family. The November 12, 1876, edition of the *Louisville Courier Journal* characterized her as a "brilliant writer, fine elocutionist, blessed with a dry droll manner, with a conundrum or story for every occasion." The author of the article noted that she had brown eyes, brown hair that hung in two long braids down her back and "the prettiest hand and foot in California" (no doubt referring to her mountain climbing abilities). Lizzie came west in 1874, not only to see the rugged frontier, but also to help ease the pains she suffered due to rheumatism. She lived in Santa Barbara for more than two years before traveling to Yosemite.[7]

The team of climbers that Lizzie accompanied to the top of South Dome included men who had scaled the mountain before: James Mason Hutchings (a wealthy businessman and one of Yosemite Valley's most ardent promoters) and George Anderson. George had made the climb the previous October with Sarah Dutcher, an assistant photographer from San Francisco. She had been the first female to make it to the top of South Dome.[8]

On October 10, 1876, Lizzie and the others who would be ascending South Dome, met at seven in the morning to begin their journey. After covering their arms, hands, and boots in pitch (a residue of petroleum) and double-checking their gear, the group started the climb. Lizzie described the venture in a letter to the *Pittsburgh Telegraph*. It was reprinted in the *Cincinnati Commercial* newspaper on October 18, 1876.

The morning found us on our horses, ready to start for the great South Dome, the highest goal of our ambition. As we rode up the mountain, Mr. Hutchings explained to us the manner in which the seeming invincible Dome had been conquered. "I tried," he said, "to climb it in [1859?], and persons have been trying to climb it ever since. A man came to me one day to tell me that he had been around the dome for three days, had examined it very carefully, and was satisfied he could reach the top. 'Very well,' said I, 'you plant a flag there when you get up, then come to me in the evening, and I will give you the best supper a man ever sat down to and twenty dollars besides for your day's work.' The man [agreed?], and went off, but somehow he forgot to call again.[9]

We had been riding up the mountain side while listening to this story and now came upon a little cabin in the forest, which Mr. Hutchings informed us was the home of our hero. In a moment he came out himself to greet us, and we saw a well formed man, a little above medium height, with brown hair, honest blue eyes and modest mien. He showed us the cabin which forms his dwelling place in winter, when frequently the snow is on a level with the roof. We examined, too, the long snow shoes with which he makes his way about at such times, and listened to stories of the narrow escapes he made once or twice last winter from burial under the beautiful snow. Mr. Anderson joined us here, and we rode up on the trail. Passing through the woods, we saw great numbers of wooden steps, and learned that Mr. Anderson had made about eleven hundred of these and with them expects to construct a stairway up the side of the Dome, so as to open to a greater number the glories to be seen from its summit. But twelve persons had ever stood there previously to that day, and these had been conducted by Mr. Anderson as he was now taking us.

Some four miles…at an altitude of about three thousand feet above the valley, we found ourselves at the foot of the "Shoulder", as it is termed, over which we must climb, before reaching the Dome proper. Had there been no dome, I imagine this would have looked sufficiently formidable to most of us, but it dwindled into insignificance compared with what was ahead. Besides, Mr. Hutchings, Mr. Anderson and the guide apparently thought nothing of it, so the rest of us kept our opinion to ourselves. Leaving our horses here, we began to climb over this mass of granite, stopping very frequently to rest and inflate our lungs and so avoid weariness, and become accustomed to the rarified atmosphere. The stone is crumbling away in many places, leaving a bed of gravel in its place. This is not the firmest foundation imaginable, and we held each other's hands to keep one another up. In some places it was quite steep….

We made the ascent of about one thousand feet and stood at last at the front of the so-called Dome. It is really only a half dome, and presents a perpendicular face to the valley. We were on the bulging side of it. The perpendicular height, from the shoulder to the summit, is over seven hundred feet. The rope, attached to the top of the Dome and fastened at intervals to the iron pins, is nine hundred and sixty feet long. It is a little slack, of course; I think there is about two hundred feet difference between the perpendicular height and the slope.

We did not pull ourselves by a rope up a perpendicular wall. We walked up the smooth granite side of the mountain, holding on to the rope for support; only occasionally pulling ourselves up, or crawling over a bulge in the rock. In a few places we were enabled to rest, too, by planting our feet against narrow, projecting ridges, and leaning back against the mountain wall. I did nothing more than the most of the party, and would not like to have my friends believe that any of us risked our lives for a whim. I do not see why anyone cannot make this ascent who has the physical strength and the courage to do so; had we been afraid, it would have been dangerous—but the fear would have made the danger.

I will here take the opportunity to set at rest all anxious inquirers by remarking that we "came down as we went up". In fact, we saw no choice in the matter: we did not think it would be comfortable to roll down, or safe to slide (which we did only occasionally and involuntarily), so we walked, holding the rope—perhaps a little more firmly than in the ascent. As for coming down "some easier way", as has been once or twice intelligently suggested, had there existed any easier way, we would probably have descended by it. Those who visit the valley next year will, perhaps, find that easier way in the steps which Mr. Anderson expects to put up. He told us that he hopes someday to have cars running up and down the slope, as on our own inclined plane, "so that old people may go up". I shall never be surprised to hear of anything Mr. Anderson accomplishes, but he has greater power of persuasion than most men, if he succeeds in inducing many old people to go up that place in a car.

We reached the top of the Dome about noon, finding some ten acres of rock upon which one can securely walk, but very little perfectly flat surface. We had been told that there was a flag on the summit, but had been obliged to take the statement on faith while in the valley. From the foot of the rope we had seen something like a white handkerchief fluttering in the air. We now found this to be a flag, three yards long and a yard wide. "Do you remember my pointing out a little black spot to you yesterday", asked the guide. "Yes", I replied, recalling the object, which appeared to me then about the size of a man's hat. "That was this clump of trees", he said, pointing to a group of eight pines. There are three species of pine growing here, *pinus Jeffre[y]i* [black pine], *pinus monticola* [mountain pine] and *pinus contorta* [lodgpole pine]; also a silver fern [fir!]—*picea amabilis*. A few varieties of ferns and grasses are found in the crevices of the rock.

We were interested less, however, in what was to be found on the Dome than in what might be seen from it. We were too tired at first, however, to give much heed to either, and it was not until we had rested awhile, and slaked our thirst with the snow that had to serve in lieu of water, that we began to look about us. Our first care then was to ascertain exactly how high we were, and Mr. Hutchings' barometer, which had afforded us interest and pleasure all the way, was brought into requisition to furnish the first accurate measurement of the height. "Five thousand and three feet above the valley", said Mr. Hutchings; "that is nine thousand feet above the level of the sea" [actually, about 8836 feet]. This afforded us intense satisfaction, for we all wanted it to be the even five thousand feet above the valley, and I was anxious to stand on a loftier height than I had ever before reached.

Looking around us now, we saw eighteen peaks, each of which was from one thousand to four thousand feet higher than the one on which we stood. Mr. Hutchings and the guide "knew them all by the name", and pointed them out to us. "There is Mt. Dana; we climbed that last summer. That is Mt. Lyell, at whose foot we saw a living glacier, the source of five great rivers. The Merced, which flows through the valley, is one; the Tuolumne, which we saw last week, another". "There is Monastery Peak". "That is Coliseum Point". "Over yonder is grand old Starr King between his two children, as those lesser peaks have been facetiously called".

We followed them from peak to peak, the sense of grandeur growing upon us all the time. Between those loftier ones, innumerable lesser mountains lifted their snow-crowned summits. We looked out in front of us to where the Coast Range traced its purple line upon the horizon—one hundred and fifty miles away. Then turned and gazed upon the snowy peaks bathing their white foreheads in the liquid blue of heaven. Then we cast our eyes downward into the valley and found in lake and river a clear, deep blue, which made rhyme with the blue above us. On every side, near and far, above, below and around about us, all was grandeur, all was glory. Ah, surely, there is no scene more full of matchless beauty, of overwhelming sublimity, can be found outside the Celestial City.

We walked to the edge of an overhanging rock and

looked down five thousand feet—almost a mile. Nowhere else in the Sierras can be found so high a perpendicular wall. Sitting by the flag staff, the guide fired some cartridges of giant powder. A feeble answer came to us from a party at Mirror Lake. The mountains responded grandly, one voice after another sending back the sound to us, making an echo which Mr. Hutchings and the guide, who had been among the mountains for years, pronounced the finest they had ever heard. We timed one of these echoes and between the first mountain voice and the last fifteen seconds elapsed.

We spent two or three hours upon the Dome, enjoying the magnificent view, and gathering ferns and crystals to keep among our most prized treasures, and then made a slow and wearisome descent. We reached our horses about 4 p.m., and I, for one, was too tired to eat the lunch which we had left there."

James Hutchings, one of the climbers that made the journey with Lizzie characterized the trip in a more succinctly in his book *In the Heart of the Sierras*. James simply wrote, "Miss L.E. Pershing, of Pittsburgh, Pennsylvania [Lizzie's initials were L.K.] the writer, and three others found their way to the top."[10]

According to the November 26, 1876, edition of the *San Francisco Bulletin*, the twenty-first instance of a party traversing the South Dome was memorable because one of the members of the party was a woman.

And what makes it still more interesting…she was a newspaper correspondent. There were four tourists in the party, all of whose names we were unable to learn, but the lady's name was Miss Lizzie R. Pershing, and she is a correspondent of the Pittsburgh, PA., Gazette. Miss Pershing is the second lady that has ever accomplished this undertaking, and it is but fair to state that but very few of the sterner sex have considered the glory of having climbed the dome a recompense for the dangers to be braved. After making an extraordinary climb on the ragged mountain side, the dome itself is reached, the ascent of which requires one to climb, by the air of ropes, up an almost perpendicular wall, without steps or foothold other than nature has made[,] a distance of 900 feet. These ropes extend from one staple in the rock to another, and the distance between the staple is from ten to fifty feet, according to circumstances. The fatigue of this perilous undertaking did not seem to seriously affect this brave little lady, for she returned from the valley today, looking as fresh and fair as if she had not accomplished a feat that makes her famous.

The October 21, 1876, edition of the *Christian Advocate* had a slightly different version of the story. "Miss Lizzie K. Pershing, daughter of President Pershing, of the Pittsburgh Female College, during a visit to California won quite a reputation as a letter-writer for several leading journals. She has recently returned home, and it appears that she has attained the title 'Heroine of the South Dome' of the Yosemite Valley, supposed to be six thousand feet high—a perpendicular wall. For many years persons have sought unsuccessfully to climb up, until a Scotch sailor succeeded."

Prior to climbing South Dome, Lizzie and a friend had traveled about Napa Valley in Northern California to see the natural hot springs that intermittently ejected a column of water and steam into the air. The article Lizzie wrote about the excursion entitled "A Trip to the Geyser" was published in the *National Repository Journal* in April 1877.

By 1884 Lizzie returned to her home state of Pennsylvania and accepted the position of vice president at the Pittsburgh Female College. She married attorney William C. Anderson, and the couple lived in the town of Wilkenson near Pittsburgh. He died on November 25, 1910. Lizzie died in the spring of 1937. She was eighty-three years old.[11]

Isabella Logan Leidig
Self-Sufficient Inn Keeper

N ature writer and conservationist John Muir sat alone at a table in the Leidig Hotel in Yosemite, patiently waiting for the breakfast he ordered to be served. He was a tall, gangly, bearded man deeply focused on a stack of geological surveys in front of him. The hotel kitchen doors swung open and appetizing aroma filled the dining area. Unable to concentrate on his work, John breathed in a cacophony of seasonings and spices and licked his lips.[1]

Isabella Logan Leidig proceeded out of the kitchen carrying a tray of delicious dishes and set them on John's table. A trail of delightful smells followed. Isabella placed the meal on the table as John stuffed a cloth napkin in his shirt and readied his knife and fork. He was served venison, ham and eggs, catfish, and the house specialty, mutton. Using a recipe she acquired from her native home of Scotland, Isabella cooked mutton with pearl barley, carrots, thyme, and a touch of cider. Fresh soda scones (flat bread cooked in a skillet) accompanied the lamb. John washed the meal down with a tall glass of milk and finished it off with a bowl of strawberry ice cream. After happily paying his tab the satisfied customer left the establishment with a promise that he would be back again and soon.[2]

Isabella's superb culinary and hospitality skills, combined with the hotel's location, made the business an ideal spot for visitors to Yosemite Valley to stay in 1869.[3] According to the July 20, 1871, edition of the *Mariposa Weekly Gazette* in the nearby town of Mariposa four of the five prominent hotels in Yosemite boasted "culinary artists who bent over hot wood ranges and brought forth memorable meals." "Of the four hotel keeper's wives whose cooking and housekeeping efforts, in a large measure, made their husband's enterprise successful, Isabella Leidig was one."

Isabella was known by friends and guests who patronized the Leidig Hotel as a stunning, dark-eyed woman. In 1863 she met George Frederick Leidig, a twenty-five-year-old mine hoist operator living in Princeton, California. The two quickly fell in love and eloped to San Francisco. The

Lotta Crabtree.

Mariposa Gazette reported that popular Gold Rush singer and actress Lotta Crabtree serenaded Isabella and George at the church where they were wed.[4]

George was a short, stout, ambitious German who wanted more for himself and his wife than life in the mining industry. When he was offered the chance to work in the Yosemite Valley on a section of land homesteaded by his friend John C. Lamon, he jumped at the chance. On July 1, 1864, President Abraham Lincoln signed a bill that would preserve Yosemite and the Big Tree Grove. Lamon, as well as four other men at various locations throughout the valley, was asked to vacate the land, but they refused. Lamon argued that, because he had resided there since 1856, it was legally his. Until the matter could be settled in court, he wanted to farm and cultivate the one-hundred-sixty acres of land he had claimed as his own, and add cottages and a hotel to the scenic spot he called home. He wanted George to aid him in his effort, to develop the land, build and manage the hotel.[5]

In 1866, George moved his family to the area. Isabella and George's two children, the elder all of two years old, traveled via horseback to their new residence. While Isabella settled into a cave near the site where their new home was being constructed, George plowed acreage and planted seeds.[6]

From April 1866 to 1869, George not only worked in Lamon's fields but also he and Isabella operated a hotel owned by Catherine Black. According to the Yosemite Valley guide Galen Clark's biography, the Leidigs were exceptional caretakers of the facility, which was a popular stop for travelers of all ages. He described the facility:

> It was a good hotel…only one story high, but one was comfortable. One area contained a kitchen, dining room, and barroom; the other had a parlor and several sleeping rooms. Some of the rooms were floored and had nails to hang clothes on. There were candles, a barrel of water with tin basins, a long towel on a roller at the corner of the house, and fragments of a looking glass in the bath facilities….I spent a few sleepless hour[s] fearing noises under the moss mattress to be a snake. Close examination disclosed a setting hen under the bed!
>
> The table was first-rate, with the juiciest and tenderest [sic] of mutton from Leidig's own flock of sheep, fresh trout from the Merced River, excellent vegetables, plenty of fruit and berries, and the richest of cream, with good cooking and neat service.[7]

Not satisfied with managing someone else's hotel, the Leidigs wanted to start their own business. George obtained a lease from the Yosemite Valley Commissioners (a board made up of geologists, politicians, and explorers, designed to act in the best interest of the park for both preservation and tourism) to operate a hotel. Completed in 1870, Leidig's Hotel was a two-story structure located near the foot of the Four Mile Trail. A view of Yosemite Falls could be seen from the porch on the first floor and balconies on the second floor.[8]

In addition to the hotel, George built a log home for Isabella and their children north of the Merced River. Shortly after they moved into it, their daughter Agnes and son McCoy ate some peaches that had gone bad. The siblings died and were buried beside one another beneath an oak tree.

Despondent over the passing of her children, Isabella withdrew from any activity but that of handling her daily chores. She washed and ironed the cotton sheets used as room partitions, stuffed the hotel mattresses with staghorn lichen (a type of fungus that grows with algae and is found on tree trunks), and perfected various dishes to serve hungry guests. Patrons with a keen appreciation of Isabella's cooking helped her through the difficult time. Their compliments inspired her to make the business the best in the valley. She transformed the fresh milk from their

Sentinel Rock looms over the Leidig Hotel.

herd of cows, fresh eggs from their free-range chickens, and mountain trout caught by George from the Merced River into choice entrees.[9]

Among the many patrons that stayed at Leidig's Hotel were author and suffragette Caroline M. Churchill, author Nathaniel Hawthorne, and lecturer and reporter Ralph Waldo Emerson. According to the book *Yosemite* by Margaret Sanborn, Emerson was struck by the hotel's beautiful setting, neat appearance, and interesting boarders. "Its' [sic] tidy arrangements," she wrote, "proved simple indeed. I was awakened in the morning by a cackling hen walking over my bed in search of a good place to lay her egg."[10]

A number of couples held their weddings and receptions at Leidig's Hotel. Guests were served a variety of items for their celebratory meals: freshly grown vegetables, cuts from the finest beef, and berry jam filled tarts. For breakfast, newlyweds could feast on catfish, mush (cornbread boiled in water or milk), and ice cream.[11]

Caroline Churchill praised the business in an article she contributed to a Denver newspaper, the *Colorado Antelope*, on September 12, 1879. "Leidig's is the best place in the line of hotels. Mrs. Leidig attends to the cooking in person; the results are that the food is well cooked and intelligently served. There is not the variety to be obtained here as in places more accessible to market. After traveling a few months in California, a person is liable to think less of variety and more of quality."

Churchill's sole criticism about the establishment was about the number of children that either lived at or hung around the hotel. Three months after Isabella and George lost their two children, Isabella became pregnant with a third. The Leidigs' son Charles was born in 1869. He was the first white boy born in Yosemite Valley. During the next eighteen years that the Leidigs owned and operated their hotel, Isabella gave birth to eight additional children. In addition to the Leidig children playing around the property, there were a number of Native American children as well. Churchill referred to them all as "beautiful, but loud and sadly neglected."[12]

According to a report entitled An Investigation of the Yosemite Commissioners, the Leidig children and their friends were far from being neglected. They were "well-fed, scrubbed, doctored, and loved."[13] Isabella not only showered her own children with attention but attended to the Indian children, too. She gave them treats for helping her with her chores and treated their scrapes and cuts and bruises with home remedies. Native children sought

Isabella's help for a variety of ailments. A young boy named Sam Wells was bitten by a rattlesnake when he came to her for a cure. His foot was severely swollen from the bite. Isabella heated a pail of milk and placed the boy's foot in the liquid. She kept the substance hot by dropping rocks pulled from a fire into it. Sam survived without incident and from that point on he called Isabella "Grandmama."[14]

Isabella Dennison, the wife of one of the heads of the Yosemite Valley Commission, W.E. Dennison, told a reporter for the July 20, 1881, edition of the *Mariposa Gazette* that "Isabella Leidig did all the work around the fourteen room hotel, restaurant, and homestead. She cared for numerous children and never had a doctor."

She was a self-reliant woman who delivered each one of her babies by herself. According to an interview with one of her relatives, Elizabeth McCauley Meyer, in July 1948 for the book *Pioneers in Petticoats*, Meyer shared that "Isabella didn't even use an Indian mid-wife when she went into labor. On one occasion, George didn't even know she had given birth. He came into the kitchen for coffee," Meyer explained, "and Isabella said, "see what I have—a blanket with a baby in it—my baby!"[15]

Isabella's hospitality attracted numerous sojourners to the Leidig Hotel. In January 1878 explorer and author A.P. Vivian was a guest at Leidig's and noted in his journal the entire family was welcoming. "Our host was glad enough to us, for tourists are very scarce commodities at this time of the year, and he determined to celebrate our arrival by exploding a dynamic cartridge [similar to a firecracker], that we might at the same time enjoy the grand echoes made in the Yosemite mountain canyon. There were doubtless extraordinary, but I am free to confess I would rather have gone away without hearing them than have experienced the anxiety of mind, and real risk to body, which preceded the pleasure."[16]

There were times when the Leidigs had to rescue paying customers who got lost hiking the trails around their hotel. Such was the case with a member of Ralph Waldo Emerson's party in 1881. According to Harvard professor James Bradley Thayer's memoirs "a well-known English woman, Mrs. Yelverton detoured from the trail and got lost in an unexpected snow storm. She was rescued with some difficulty by Leidig, our landlord. Mrs. Leidig helped the frightened hiker recover from the ordeal with a well prepared meal."[17]

Isabella acquired the majority of her supplies for her family and the hotel guests from stores in San Francisco. The items were delivered by a pack train of thirty or forty animals.[18]

After eighteen years operating the Leidig Hotel, Isabella, George, and all but one of their nine children relocated to the town of Raymond in Madera County, California. George worked as a hotel keeper there and Isabella cooked for guests and the children who still lived at home. The Leidigs heard often from their son Charles, who had remained in the valley. He became a government ranger and an avid fisherman, providing the hotels and businesses with trout. He served as a guide to President Theodore Roosevelt when the politician visited the valley in 1903.[19]

The Leidig Hotel, as well as the Sentinel Hotel nearby, was demolished when a more modern hotel was built in the national park in 1888. Only a handful of locust trees mark the site of what was once the center of pioneer activity.[20]

George Leidig died on June 13, 1902, from cirrhosis of the liver. He was laid to rest at the Arbor Vitae Cemetery in Raymond. Isabella died on June 27, 1923, at the home of one of her daughters in Fresno, California. She was seventy-six years old.[21]

Isabella Leidig's Scottish Mutton Recipe

Take a loin of mutton, cut it into small chops, season with ground pepper, all spice and salt; let it stand a night and then fry it. Have good gravy, well-seasoned with flour, butter, catsup and pepper, if necessary. Boil turnips and carrots, cut them small, and add to mutton, stew in the gravy with the yokes of hard-boiled eggs, and forcemeat balls. Some great pickles will be an improvement.[22]

Maggie Howard
Paiute Basket Maker and Teacher

The dark clouds that hovered over a crude trail in Yosemite Valley in May 1899 broke loose with a torrent of rain that nearly knocked Paiute Indian Maggie "Ta-bu-ce" Howard and her fourteen-year-old niece, May Tom, off the rocky path where they walked. Mighty claps of thunder echoed around the majestic granite walls of Yosemite Falls, and huge boulders shook from the sound. A powerful wind charged down the mountain and tossed leaves, twigs, and brush into the air. Maggie and May Tom hurried to an outcropping of craggy rocks and huddled underneath them. Lightning flashed violently, and the wind raged on without ceasing. It was as if the sky just beyond their crude shelter was in an angry pursuit to destroy them.[1]

As soon as the rain eased a bit, the pair raced toward a grove of trees, and there they made camp. The following morning they had planned to travel to their home in Indian Village along the Merced River. In spite of the wind and continual rain, Maggie and May Tom eventually managed to fall asleep. Their uneasy slumber was interrupted sometime in the night by a massive pine tree that blew over on them. May Tom was killed instantly. Maggie's collar bone was broken; the bones in her right leg were fractured, and her ankles and feet were severely injured.[2] When the two didn't arrive home the evening of the storm, worried relatives went in search of Maggie and her niece. They were heartbroken by what they saw. May Tom's mother and brothers took her body back to the valley where they lived, and Maggie was transported to a doctor. He set her bones in casts that extended over most of her frame. She was unable to move until the bones mended in late August. Maggie couldn't recall anything after the tree hit her, but the lifetime limp she acquired as a result of her injury served as a reminder of the events leading up to the tragedy.[3]

Naturalist and explorer John Muir referred to the storms that occurred at Yosemite as "not easily borne." Maggie was in complete agreement. According to the June 3, 1910, edition of the Hayward, California, newspaper the *Hayward Daily Review*, it is estimated that Maggie "Ta-bu-ce" Howard was born in 1867 at Mono Lake thirteen miles east of Yosemite Valley. She was a Paiute Indian and her name Ta-bu-ce meant "grass nut" or "sweet-root." Her father, Joaquin Sam, or Kosana as his tribe called him, was a medicine man who made frequent trips to Yosemite to gather acorns and piñon nuts. He would bring them home to Maggie's mother, who ground them into flour for bread-making. Kosana passed away at the age of eighty while en route home from Yosemite Valley. A snowstorm overtook the group of Indians he was traveling with, and they were unable to make it over the Sierra Mountains before Kosana died from exposure. He was buried near what is now the Yosemite Museum.[4]

When Maggie grew up, she moved to the area where her father had made many pilgrimages. She lived in the Indian village at the mouth of Indian Canyon. Maggie worked as housekeeper and cook at the Sentinel Hotel in 1877. The Sentinel, only a year old then, was one of the first hotels in Yosemite. It was owned by James Mason Hutchings and his family. After several years in their employ, Maggie became an independent contractor as a maid and cook for prominent area families.[5]

Away from her day job, Maggie practiced and lived out the traditions she learned from her Paiute ancestors. She prepared meals they originated, which consisted of acorn-water biscuits and porridge made with powdered acorns and seasoned with insect pupae known as *ka-cha-vee*. She cooked all her food with heated rocks, added, with water, to leakproof baskets called *hikis*. Maggie made the baskets herself.

According to the October 29, 1931, edition of the Mariposa County, California, newspaper the *Mariposa Gazette*, acorns were a main staple

Maggie Howard gathers acorns in baskets she made herself. COURTESY OF YOSEMITE NPS LIBRARY

of the Paiute Indian diet. It was a source of food the Native Americans never worried would disappear. "The acorn crop is usually bountiful and they [the Indians] gather large supplies which they then grind into meal and make into nutritious 'bread' and 'mush'. the Indians filled sack after sack with the nuts of the black oak. When Maggie was questioned as to how she would manage to eat so many acorns, she replied, "I eat plenty. Some I take to my family at Mono Lake. No oak trees at Mono Lake—no acorns at Mono Lake."[6] The acorn bread Maggie made was not only used in her daily meal, but was also sold to Yosemite visitors.

Maggie's skills at basket weaving were exceptional. She interlaced strips of American dogwood, big-leaf maple, buck-brush, deer-brush, willow, and California hazelnut together to make containers of various shapes and sizes. Pieces of blackened fern were added to the basket for color. Women like Maggie knew the names of all the plants for basketmaking, where to find them, and the best time to gather them. She also knew how to prepare these for weaving. The plant materials had to be peeled, trimmed to correct width, fineness, and length, soaked in cold water, and boiled or buried in mud, according to their use.[7]

Among the type of baskets made were large conical shaped baskets known as burden baskets. They were used to carry heavy and bulky loads. These baskets were supported on the back by a strap passing over the wearer's forehead.[8]

Visitors to Yosemite could not resist hiking or riding to Indian Village to admire Maggie's baskets and learned about life in the valley. She was happy to answer all questions posed about her work, the meals she made from acorns, and the customs of the Paiute people. She would allow

Maggie Howard prepares acorns for use, in a demonstration at the Yosemite Museum.
Courtesy of Yosemite NPS Library

pictures to be taken of her if she was politely asked and adequately paid. She resented tourists who snapped a photograph without permission and then hurried away without giving her any money for the privilege.[9]

Maggie sustained herself on a modest income made from the sale of her baskets, and tips from visitors who appreciated the lectures she delivered about Yosemite. She was good at watching her money and prided herself on being thrifty. She managed to save $1,800. She spent nearly twenty years interpreting Pauite life to Yosemite park guests.[10]

In 1939 Maggie traveled to San Francisco to take advantage of the offer an ophthalmologist made to remove cataracts on both eyes. Newspaper reporters and cameramen, hearing of the Indian woman's first trip to a major city, turned out in droves at the railroad depot to capture the momentous occasion. Maggie was overwhelmed by the crowd, traffic, and imposing buildings. The flash from the cameras added to her anxiety, and she barely made it to the Stanford University Hospital before collapsing from the pressure.[11]

Maggie recuperated from the surgery at a friend's home in Albany,

Ta-bu-ce, Maggie Howard, with a traditional acorn-storage structure.
COURTESY OF YOSEMITE NPS LIBRARY

California, before returning to Yosemite to continue healing. Although the cataracts had been removed, Maggie's eyesight was far from being perfect. She was fitted for two pairs of glasses, one to help with her nearsightedness and the other to assist with farsightedness. She struggled with knowing which pair to wear when. She worried that she would never be able to get it straight and never be able to see well enough to take up basketmaking again. The cost for the glasses, hospital stay, and operation contributed to Maggie's despair. She was concerned about how she was going to make a living. It wasn't until the surgeon made it clear that he was paying for the procedure and subsequent care that Maggie felt any kind of relief.[12]

By the summer of 1940, Maggie's good health had been restored and she was back to her daily routine at Indian Village. She entertained thousands of park visitors with demonstrations of authentic Indian life and customs. Stationed under an oak tree, she would pound acorns, sift the meal, pour it into a sand basin, leach out the bitter tannic acid, and bake small acorn cakes. She also made beaded jewelry.[13]

Life passed calmly for Maggie until World War II. Frightened by the news, she left Yosemite to be near her sons, Willie Mike Williams and Simon "Slim" Lundy, both living at Mono Lake. Maggie had been married three times. Her first husband was Jack Lundy, her second Billy Williams, and third was Dan Howard.[14]

Maggie's Native American religious beliefs were very important to her. Prior to every meal she offered prayers to the animal gods she believed watched over her and her children. She believed witches could seek people out to do harm. Maggie often relayed a story to friends about a witch that tormented her. The witch placed a rock inside Maggie that made her ill. The rock was eventually removed by a medicine man. Maggie told how the medicine man chanted, prayed, and waved his hand over her body before extracting the offensive rock.[15]

Maggie Howard passed away on January 25, 1947. Historians speculate the woman known as the first Indian demonstrator in Yosemite was over ninety. According to the February 2, 1947, edition of the *Nevada State Journal*, Maggie died of natural causes near tribal grounds at Mono Lake.

The burial ceremony was in keeping with the tradition of Maggie's Paiute ancestors. Relatives and friends sang and danced around her body as she was laid to rest. The *Nevada State Journal* noted that "Maggie's passing severed one of the last links in the chain which connects the present with the days when Indians roamed the valleys and mountains free from restraint of the white man."

In addition to the impact Maggie had in sharing Native American culture with tourists who traveled to Yosemite, she was remembered by all who knew her personally as "dignified, self-sufficient, and always of good cheer."[16]

The Paiute Process of Making Acorn Meal

The way to make acorn meal, which removed the nut's bitter taste, was also handed down from generation to generation. Maggie Howard started with one cup acorn-meal, one teaspoon of salt, two and a half cups of water, one teaspoon honey or sugar, and one eighth cup of hickory nuts or black walnuts, crushed. Then she boiled the water with the salt. After adding the acorn meal, she boiled the mixture for fifteen minutes, then removed from the heat and allowed it to cool for about five minutes. Finally, she stirred in the honey and nuts.[17]

Maggie Howard's Acorn Bread

Two cups of acorn meal, half cup of milk (or water), one tablespoon of baking powder, two cups of wheat flour, three tablespoons of butter or olive oil, one egg. Add a third of a cup honey or maple syrup or sugar, if available. Combine all the above ingredients and pour into a loaf pan. Bake at four hundred degrees for thirty minutes or until done. Yields a moist bread with a sweet, nutty flavor.[18]

Louisa Strentzel Muir

Naturalist's Mainstay

The light from a spectacular full moon spilled into the windows of the parlor at the Strentzel Ranch near the town of Martinez in the Alhambra Valley in California. The room was filled to overflowing with well dressed guests, owners and operators of farms in the area and their wives and families. All eyes were on Louisa "Louie" Wanda Strentzel, a petite, thirty-one-year-old woman playing a piano. No one spoke as the melancholy tune she offered filled the air. Louie played well and had a voice to match. Midway through the mesmerizing performance, forty-year- old John Muir, an explorer and naturalist from Wisconsin, quietly entered the home and stood in the shadow of the door leading into the parlor. With the exception of a quiet greeting from Strentzel family friend Mrs. Jeanne Carr, his presence went largely unnoticed.[1]

John's eyes were transfixed on Louie. She had high cheek bones, a firm mouth, and clear, gray eyes. He gazed at her with an unfathomable look of admiration and longing. At the conclusion of her song the gathering enthusiastically applauded. John followed suit as he ventured into the light. It was June 1, 1878.[2]

This was not the first time he had seen Louie. The two had been introduced in 1874 in Oakland at a meeting of homesteaders and farmers organized by her father, horticulturist Dr. John Strentzel. John Muir and Louie Strentzel had quite a few friends in common, and many agreed they would make the perfect couple. Jeanne Carr had tried in vain to arrange a date between them, but Muir always had travel plans that conflicted with a rendezvous. In April 1875 Jeanne sent Louie a message letting her known that the "chronic wanderer," as John was often referred to, could not be distracted from an expedition to the Cascade Range in Siskiyou County, California. "You see how I am snubbed in trying to get John Muir to accompany me to your house this week," Jeanne wrote Louie. "Mount Shasta was in opposition and easily worth the choice." Jeanne would not be defeated, however. She was convinced the two had so much in common their paths were bound to pass eventually and forever.[3]

Louie Strentzel was born in Texas in 1847. She was an only child and, according to Louie and John's daughter, Helen, "she was a devoted daughter and a great comfort to her parents in their later years." Her father, a Polish physician who fled to American in 1840 to escape being drafted into the Russian Army, settled in the southwest near the city now known as Dallas. In 1849, he left Texas for California. Strentzel moved his wife and child to the Alhambra Valley north of Oakland. He purchased several hundred acres of land and began educating himself on how to grow various crops. According to the May 5, 1974, edition of the Joplin, Missouri, newspaper *Joplin Grove*, the main product at the Strentzel farm was peaches.[4]

Louie inherited her father's love of plants and flowers. In addition to her affection for growing things, she was interested in astronomy, poetry, and music. She was extremely bright and excelled at her studies at Miss Adkins' Young Ladies Seminary in Benicia. Louie became a music scholar while attending the school, and her teachers boasted that she had a bright future as a concert pianist if she so chose. Once she graduated in 1864 she decided to return home to the ranch in Martinez and focus on fruit ranching and hybridizing.[5]

The stunning and talented Louie was not only the pride of her family, but according to the January 5, 1975, edition of the Long Beach, California, newspaper *Independent Press Telegram*, "she was known widely for the grace with which she dispensed the generous hospitality of the Strentzel household."

John Muir was a frequent guest at the Strentzel homestead. He enjoyed conversing with Dr. Strentzel about his trek from Texas to California. Strentzel had been the medical advisor for a wagon train of pioneers called the Clarkesville Train. He had kept a journal of his travels and happily shared the experience with John. The Spanish name for the Alhambra Valley where the Strentzels settled was "Canada de la Hambre." The English translation being Valley of Hunger. "Mrs. Strentzel was displeased with the name," the doctor informed John. "Remembering [author Washington] Irving's glowing description of the Moorish paradise, I decided to re-christen our home Alhambra after the palace at Granada Spain." Strentzel's interest in plants and raising crops best suitable for the terrain prompted him to grow citrus fruit on the more than six hundred acres he had purchased.[6]

Although he appreciated farming, John's main interest at the time was the exploration of the western territories of the United States. According to Louie's mother, Louisianna, John was "shy and quiet." When he wasn't hiking across the mountains of Northern California or embarking on wilderness adventures through Alaska, he spent time in the Alhambra Valley learning about agriculture.[7]

It wasn't until the summer of 1878 that John saw Louie as more than just the daughter of the man he admired. The two began a courtship that lasted more than a year. They were polar opposites in many ways. John was outgoing, and Louie was timid. Her manner of dress was prim and proper, and John's look was disheveled and like a field worker. Louie was a member of the Methodist church and regularly attended. John did not. They did share a love of botany, astronomy, politics, and current affairs. "Mr. Muir is the only man that the Dr. and I ever felt that we could take into our family as one of us," Louisianna

Strentzel wrote in her journal, "and he is the only one that Louie has ever loved, although she has had many offers of marriage. O, can we ever feel thankful enough to God for sending us this man."[8]

The day after the couple announced their intent to marry, John left on a trip to Alaska. While he was discovering ancient glaciers, Louie was planning their nuptials, planting a variety of flowers, and tending to a vegetable garden. The two exchanged numerous letters. John wrote his fiancee about how he made his way through part of the region in a dugout canoe using members of the Tlingit Indian tribe as his guide. Louie, who was overcome with worry for her betrothed's safety on the trip, crept into her parents' room at one o'clock in the morning to tell her mother the good news. "Louie came to me, overcome with emotion, threw her arms around me and said, 'O, mother, all is well…,'" Louisianna Strentzel included in her journal.[9]

In another letter John wrote to Louie in October 1879, he shared with her the spectacular beauty of the frozen terrain he was exploring. "Every summer my gains from God's wilds grow greater. This last seems the greatest of all. For the last few weeks I was so feverishly excited with the boundless exuberance of the woods and the wilderness, of great ice floods, and the manifest scriptures of the ice-sheet that modeled the lovely archipelagoes along the coast, that I could hardly settle down to the steady labor required in making any sort of truth one's own. But I'm working now, and feel unable to leave the field. Had a most glorious time of it among the glaciers…"[10]

John returned to California in early 1880, and he and Louie were married on April 14 that same year. The two exchanged vows at her parents' home, before a makeshift altar decorated with white Astrakhan apple blossoms.[11]

According to the January 5, 1976, edition of the *Independent Press Telegram*, John suspended his personal exploration journeys from August 1881 to March 1889. He decided to stay put and write about his recent travels, and to manage the Strentzel's large fruit ranch. On March 25, 1881, Louie gave birth to their first child, a daughter they named Wanda.

Five years later the Muirs had another daughter, Helen. She was born on January 23, 1886.[12]

In addition to raising their children, Louie and John raised a variety of apples, peaches, grapes, and cherries on the farm. John used the vast agricultural knowledge he acquired attending Wisconsin University and through his extensive travels to cultivate plants that ripened early and lasted beyond their season. The Muirs diligence and innovation resulted in substantial profits for the ranch. It was John's goal to earn enough money to support his family when he returned to his life's work, which he considered to be conservation. Louie was in favor of his returning to the wilderness to study. The *Independent Press Telegram* article reported that Louie recognized John was not delighted with the routine of ranch work. She knew it was not his life's dream to supervise the forty-plus Chinese laborers employed by the Strentzel Ranch. She also knew John would never be completely happy unless he was able to spend time in solitude in the mountains.

John usually entertained thoughts of travel between July and October while the grapes ripened and there was a lull in ranch work. In the eight years he had devoted himself entirely to the ranch, he had earned more than $100,000. In July 1888, Louie urged John to "throw some tea and bread in a sack, jump over the back fence, and take up his studies of the wild again." Fortified by her unselfish gesture, he bade the family farewell and made his way to Washington's Mount Rainer.[13]

Any doubts John might have had about continuing his trek through the Northwest were set to rest by a letter from his wife, while he was in Seattle, dated August 9, 1888. "Dear John, a ranch that needs and takes the sacrifice of a noble life, or work, ought to be flung away beyond all reach…," Louie wrote,

> The Alaska book and Yosemite book, Dear John, must be
> written, and you need to be your own self, well and strong
> to make them worthy of you. There is nothing that has a
> right to be considered besides this except the welfare of our
> children.[14]

According to Louie and John's daughter Helen, her mother worked hard to maintain the ranch in her father's absence. She preferred home life over traveling. Staying in rustic hotels while en route to out of the way locations made her uncomfortable. Louie enjoyed ranch living and, with the help of the ranch foreman, was able to make sure the cultivating and planting was done in the spring. John would return by the fall to harvest the crops. When Louie wasn't overseeing the daily duties at the ranch, she was working on her garden around the farm house. "Mama loved flowers, especially fragrant ones," Helen recalled in her memoirs about her parents. "Of course, there were roses of all kinds, but the great thicket of single Cherokee roses were by far the sweetest; and there were jasmine, honeysuckle, lavender, lilies, wisteria, magnolias, and heliotrope."[15]

Louie accompanied John only once to Yosemite, in 1884, and the trip proved to be a regrettable one for both. She did not like hiking, had no aptitude for fishing, and was terrified of being attacked by bears. John felt Louie overpacked for the expedition and was annoyed with having to take her numerous trunks of clothes with them.[16]

Louie was content reading John's letter about his travels. He offered brilliant descriptions of the locales, and Louie could envision the spots without the distraction of luggage, crude transportation, and wild animals. "Sunshine dear Louie," John wrote his wife from St. Michael's, Alaska, on June 21, 1881.

> ...sunshine all the day, ripe, mellow, sunshine, like that
> which feeds the fruits vines. It came to us just [illegible]
> days ago when we were approaching this little old fashioned
> trading post at the mount of the Yukon River. How sweet
> kindly reviving it is after so long deep a burial beneath dark
> sleety storm clouds.[17]

When John had encountered the spectacular Yosemite landscape for the first time in 1868, his plan had been to familiarize himself with every mountain peak, waterfall, and canyon. In order to fulfill his objective and support himself financially, he worked as a shepherd leading livestock through the alpine meadows. He hired on at a saw mill, too, and studied the giant trees from the Mariposa Grove that had fallen naturally, trees he would use to build cabins for hikers.[18]

John's desire to explore and research the vast region only increased after he and Louie married. When she sent him off to the Sierras in 1888, her only request was that he would supply her and their children with sketches of the area, samples of flora, and specific information about the fields and mountains that could be passed on from one generation to another. John was happy to comply and moved to preserve the integrity of Yosemite not only for his daughters, but also for the nation as well. From the tiny trails maintained by grasshoppers and the birds that took up residence in the forests, to the measurement of the rain and snow

Helen, Wanda, Louie, and John Muir at home on their ranch.
COURTESY OF THE NATIONAL PARK SERVICE, JOHN MUIR NHS, JOMU1742

and how thunder echoed in the rocky canyons, John never failed to record his findings. It was largely due to his dedication to documenting nature and his drive to keep the land intact that led government officials to make Yosemite a National Park in 1890.[19] Its boundaries were based on John's recommendation. "I am bewitched and enchanted by Yosemite Valley's allure," he wrote in a letter to Louie in October 1890. He was convinced that the region was "not valuable for any other use than the use of beauty." The published article he wrote about his venture, called "The Century," echoed the sentiment he had so long shared with his wife.[20]

According to Louie and John's older daughter, Helen, life at home with her parents was happy. "Mama was the perfect helpmate," she told a reporter with the *Pasadena Star-News* in May 1963. "My father's interest and lifework became my mother's own lifework too and she did all she could, gladly and willingly, to help him." When John returned home from Yosemite in early 1891, he spent time working on his first book, entitled *The Mountains of California*. Louie made sure nothing interrupted John's writing, including her piano playing. "Papa could not endure piano music while he was writing," Helen told a *Martinez Patch* reporter. "His study was directly over the parlor where the piano stood. Mama understood and did not play for my sister and me."[21]

According to Helen, Louie was very well read. She enjoyed books and newspaper articles about inventions and inventors and was particularly fond of two specific magazines, *Review of Reviews* and *World's Work*. Both focused on the academic world and individuals who aspired to make changes politically and in education. John valued Louie's opinion and had her review everything he wrote. He thought she was a "most intelligent woman" and said she was his "most trusted critic and advisor," as their daughter told the *Pasadena Star News*. Louie reviewed the books John wrote as well as the petitions he penned for charter members of the Sierra Club, an environmental organization founded in 1892 by Muir, artist William Keith, journalist Robert Underwood, and several Stanford University professors, to name a few.[22]

Louie was responsible for teaching Wanda and Helen reading, writing, math, history, and religion. John took charge of teaching the girls about nature. He referred to it in his memoirs as "wild knowledge." "Less arithmetic and grammar, keeps the heart alive, nourishes youth's enthusiasms, which in society die untimely," he insisted.[23]

At the end of a work day or at home after a long journey through the Sierras, John always made time to join Louie in playing with their children. They enjoyed a variety of outdoor games, and especially liked listening to John tell stories about bears, wolves, and deer, and his encounters with them. "Father [was] the biggest, jolliest child of us all," Helen remembered about her father to the *Pasadena Star News*.

In the spring of 1893, John traveled to Europe to study the glacial fjords of Norway and Switzerland, the mountains of northern Italy, and the lakes of Killarney in Ireland. His absence was keenly felt by his daughters and Louie. The couple exchanged numerous letters expressing their feelings and sharing information about home and trip through foreign lands. "Your charming letters…have been read and enjoyed by all the family, and oh how well all wanted to be there with you," Louie wrote to John in June 1893. "The magnolias are in bloom here, to the children's delight," she added. "Wanda and Helen will write tomorrow. Many kisses and much love from us all."[24]

Between 1894 and 1903, John and Louie celebrated the release of two books John wrote, *The Mountains of California* and *Our National Parks*. The cherry and peach crops grown at the Strentzel Ranch were bountiful; Louie finally had the music room soundproofed, and their daughters completed school.[25]

On May 15, 1903, John Muir was en route to the Yosemite Valley with the governor of California, George Pardee, and President Theodore Roosevelt. The president wanted to know more about the Yosemite area and requested that John escort him around. John hoped President Roosevelt would approve a grant to fund the management and upkeep of the national park. The trip was a success. Roosevelt agreed that Yosemite needed constant care and protection from visitors who mistreated the land. John then shifted his focus to Congress and trying to persuade them to accept the idea. During the legislative process, John received news from home that Louie was desperately ill.[26]

John was by Louie's side when she passed away from lung cancer on August 6, 1905. She was fifty-eight years old. Her death devastated John. Friends close to the Muirs described her as "the mainstay of the Muir household" and noted that "if not for her understanding and willingness to unselfishly forgo demands on John's time, the work he did for Yosemite Valley might have been diminished." John regarded Louie as a "loving, sympathetic wife." "We all grieved for her," Helen told said.[27]

Louie was buried in the Strentzel-Muir Cemetery a mile from the family's ranch home. John died on December 24, 1914, of pneumonia, and his body was laid to rest next to Louie's.[28]

Sarah Dutcher & Lady Jane Franklin

Daring Lady-Tourists

Yosemite National Park's Half Dome, the hooded monk in stone brooding over the park's eastern end, rises thousands of feet from the valley, so high that its summit is wreathed in clouds. In October 1876, three men scaled the mountain face, slowly working their way to the top. All were dressed in woolen caps and trousers, thick coats and gloves, and leather boots. Scotsman George Anderson, a former sailor and carpenter working in Yosemite Valley as a blacksmith and surveyor, led the way up the massive rock. The confident manner in which he ascended the mountain suggested he was a seasoned climber. Author Julius Birge followed closely behind George, his face a mask of strained concentration and worry that confirmed he was a novice at climbing. Occasional gusts of wind tried to knock the men off balance, but they persevered, finding finger hold after finger hold, and finally pulling themselves onto a ledge at the top. The second adventure seeker with the party proceeded behind him trying to regain his strength.[1]

Resting on the summit, the men stared out over the valley admiring the scenic grandeur. Yosemite Valley had an average width of half a mile. The great walls of the canyons all around them were seamed by

water-worn fissures, down which rivers leapt, thundered, churned, and sang with all possible variations and expressions of sound.[2]

In his memoirs entitled *Awakening in the Desert* published in 1912, Julius described the process of arriving at the top of Half Dome. "Anderson had spent the summer drilling holes into the granite face of the upper cliff," he wrote. "Driving in it iron pins with ropes attached. Two or three were tempted to scale with the aid of these ropes the heights which are nearly a perpendicular mile. I, too, was inclined to make the venture. It was a dizzy but inspiring ascent."[3]

After more than an hour at Half Dome's summit, catching his breath and preparing himself for the desert, Julius found an unusual item on the rocks. "I discovered on its barren surface a lady's bracelet," he recalled in his book. "On showing it to Anderson, he said: You are the third party who has made this ascent. I pulled up a young woman recently but she never mentioned any loss except for nausea. Returning to Merced, I observed a vigorous, young woman wearing a bracelet similar to the one I found. The lady proved to be Miss Sally Dutcher of San Francisco, who admitted to the loss and thankfully accepted the missing ornament. A letter to me from Galen Clark (Yosemite resident, businessman, and explorer) stated that he assisted in Miss Dutcher's ascent, Anderson preceding with a rope around his waist connecting with Miss Dutcher; also that she was certainly the first and possibly the last woman who made the ascent."[4]

Although the exact date is not known, Sarah Louisa Dutcher was the first woman to make her way to the top of Half Dome. Historians believe the intrepid young woman accomplished the feat in 1875.[5] According to James Hutchings, a British-immigrant journalist who supported Yosemite protections and wrote about his travels there, "Miss S.L. Dutcher was the first lady that ever stood upon the mountain. George Anderson was one of the first human beings to ascend Half Dome and his efforts made it possible for others to follow." "In preparation for the climb," James wrote in his memoirs, "Anderson's next efforts were directed toward placing and securely fastening a good, soft rope to the eye-bolts, so others could climb up and enjoy the inimitable view, and one that has

In a photograph taken by her employer, Carleton Watkins, Sally Dutcher wears a Bloomer costume. The overskirt hides below-the-knee Turkish trousers. COURTESY OF THE CALIFORNIA HISTORY ROOM, CALIFORNIA STATE LIBRARY, SACRAMENTO

WATKINS' YOSEMITE ART GALLERY, Portrait and Landscape, 26 Montgomery Street, opp. L'ck House Entr

not its counterpart on earth. Four English gentlemen, then sojourning in the valley and learning of Mr. Anderson's feat, were induced to duplicate his intrepid example. A day or two afterwards, Sarah Dutcher, with the courage of a heroine, accomplished it."[6]

Sarah Dutcher, or Sallie as she preferred to be called, was born in Tasmania on September 14, 1844. Her parents, Moses A. Dutcher and Sarah Burchill, were originally from England but were banished to Australia in 1839 for challenging the British government's rule over Canada, and participating in what was known as the Patriot's War. Sarah was the first of the couple's four children.[7]

In 1851 the Dutchers moved to Honolulu, Hawaii, and opened a boarding house. Sarah was eighteen when she left the Hawaiian Islands for San Francisco. She was charming and personable and became very much a part of San Francisco's social scene. She was a frequent guest at prestigious parties hosted by influential people in state politics, such as San Francisco Mayor Henry Frederick Teschamacher and agricultural business leaders such as William Hollister.[8] Newspapers often reported on Sarah's presence at various elite events. An article in the September 11, 1868, edition of the *San Francisco Daily Evening Bulletin* noted that "she attended the Carnival Ball at the Pavillion" and "received a very warm reception." "Miss Salle Dutcher was a very charming, pleasant girl, in a blue shirt, white waist, coquettish apron, and skirt," the story continued. Sarah was described by most party goers as a "lithe, remarkably self-possessed young woman, with piercing black eyes, and a face brim full of vivacity."

By April 1874, Sarah was working as a sales representative for popular photographer Carleton Watkins. Carleton made his name photographing majestic locations around California. He was the first to turn the camera straight up and shoot. Patrons of his work included Yosemite park proponent and wife of explorer John C. Fremont, Jessie Fremont.[9] Sarah represented Carleton's work in the Yosemite Valley. According to the March 14, 1880, edition of the *New York Tribune*, Sarah was one of two aggressive sales women in the region. She was the more popular of the pair, and was regarded as an expert on Carleton and photography. "A brace of female agents of photographic views infest the hotels in Yosemite Valley," the *New York Tribune* article announced, "one is well-known to every dweller in the valley by the name of 'Sally'. Great is the power of her tongue. To clinch a bargain, she will chat, flirt, dance, drive with you—a most 'amoosin' and versatile girl. Old residents of the valley remark to newcomer, with a knowing wink, as she passes: 'There goes Sally. That gal is the smartest salesman in California....She's a credit to the state, and the valley is proud of her.'"

Sarah's main competitor was a representative of East Coast photography. When the two arrived at a hotel in Yosemite at the same time, they sparred verbally to see who would call on the business owners first. "Her rival is a blonde of the 'strawberry' type, with yellow hair, who wins much custom by pertinacity and would put to shame a Niagara Falls Hackman," the *New York Tribune* report noted. "And how the two rivals do stab each other's reputations with innuendo and sarcasm: how they disparage each other's wares and make bitter gibes on mutual blemishes in beauty and honesty."

In April 1880, Sarah decided to stop selling Carleton photographs hotel-to-hotel and open her own photo gallery in San Francisco. Her business, located at 38 Montgomery Street, was listed in the city's business directory, and Sarah was referred to as an "agent for Watkins' photographic views."

Rumors circulated among San Francisco's socialites that Sarah and Carleton, who was born in November 1829, were romantically involved. Carleton's bride of six months did not react well to the insinuation, and, according to a biography of the conservation photographer, he wrote his wife several letters denying any affair.[10]

Although there was speculation and conjecture about a sexual relationship between Sarah and Carleton, there was never any question they were friends. The two took a trip through the northern California mountains to photograph the area. In addition to taking pictures of the grand scenery of the Calaveras big trees, Carleton also snapped a pair of photographs of Sarah. A close-up he took of the adventurous woman is one of most commonly used images of her.[11]

In mid-1879 Sarah met Frederick C. Clark, a topographer and meteorologist, through mutual friend Peter Palmquist, who was a correspondent for the *New York Times*. Peter introduced forty-year-old Frederick to Sarah at a party in San Francisco. He was working in the city for a branch of the United States Geological Society. Frederick was described by his geological assistant Gustavus R. Belcher as being "tall and slight with exceptional posture." He had a dark mustache and beard that he wore in an unusual way. "The beard was parted in the middle," Belcher wrote in his memoirs, "after the style of a German field marshal, and brushed so abruptly apart that each particular hair occupied at absolutely right angles to its line of natural growth. In fact, he was noticeably a-la-militaire in all his movements and appearance."[12]

Sarah and Frederick were drawn to each other because of their mutual appreciation for the outdoors. Both enjoyed traveling and hiking, and they shared affection for Yosemite Valley and the photography of Carleton Watkins. After a brief courtship the two became engaged. The *San Francisco Evening Bulletin* noted their wedding on December 18, 1880, with Rev. Dr. Scott officiating. The pair left San Francisco in 1882 and moved to Oakland, where Frederick was hired as Assistant Division Superintendent of the Central Pacific Railroad.

By the end of 1885, Sarah and Frederick's marriage was suffering. A report of their impending divorce made the December 15, 1885, edition of the *San Francisco Bulletin*. On January 9, 1886, a brief article in the *Daily Alta California* newspaper announced that their union was officially over. "Fred A. Clark has been granted a decree of divorce from Sarah L. Clarke," the notice read. Frederick remained in the Bay Area until 1904 then relocated to New York. The little information gleaned about Sarah's life ends here. Where she moved or what she did after the demise of her marriage is a mystery.

Sarah Dutcher was the first woman to climb Half Dome, but Jane Griffin Franklin was the oldest woman to venture up Vernal Falls. Lady Franklin made her way up the tremendous rock in 1863 at the age of seventy-one. She was the widow of Arctic explorer Sir John Franklin. Sir John and Lady Franklin shared a love of adventure. Not long after the two married in London in 1828 she accompanied him to Van Diemen's Land (better known as Tasmania), where he had been appointed governor over the colony.[13]

Jane Franklin in her youth.
COURTESY OF THE CALIFORNIA HISTORY ROOM, CALIFORNIA STATE LIBRARY, SACRAMENTO, CALIFORNIA

Jane was the second daughter born to Mary and John Griffin on December 4, 1805. Her parents were prosperous silk traders in London. From a very young age Jane traveled extensively throughout Europe with her family. She met her husband through a friend poet named Eleanor Anne Porden. Eleanor became Franklin's first wife. It wasn't until after Eleanor's death of tuberculosis in 1825 that John and Jane became close. The couple was married on November 5, 1828. John received a knighthood from George IV in 1829.[14]

While the Franklins were living in Tasmania, Lady Franklin helped her husband improve conditions for the natives on the island they presided over. She toured the mainland of Australia promoting the social and cultural life of Tasmania and, in so doing, became the first woman to undertake the journey from Melbourne to Sydney.[15]

In 1845, shortly after Lady Franklin and Sir John celebrated their twenty-fourth wedding anniversary, Sir John embarked upon an expedition to the polar seas. Neither Sir John nor his crew returned. It was rumored that he and his men had perished when the boat they were traveling in capsized on a rock and sank. Lady Franklin refused to accept her husband was gone. She believed he was too experienced at his job to allow anything to go wrong. Lady Franklin's name became famous because of the efforts she made to definitely determine the fate of Sir John's expedition. In London in 1848 she offered a heavy reward for trustworthy information concerning her husband and his men. The following year she made a strong appeal to the people of the United States to help in the search.[16]

Henry Grimmel of New York responded to her call for help. According to the August 5, 1875, edition of a Pennsylvania, newspaper, he purchased two ships and set out on a search sanctioned by the British government. They returned without success. Expeditions by other ambitious men like followed; the funds for each were furnished by Lady Franklin. In 1857 a ship called the *Fox* commanded by a Captain McClintock returned with proof that the unfortunate Sir John and his party had indeed perished in early 1847.[17]

Grieving over the substantiated death of her husband, Lady Jane traveled throughout the United States, visiting Alaska, California, and Nevada. She arrived in Virginia City, Nevada, in the fall of 1861. The November 23, 1890, edition of the *Salt Lake Tribune* recalled that "there were very few persons in town who weren't aware of the fact that Lady Jane Franklin, widow of Sir John Franklin, the great but unfortunate Arctic explorer, was touring the Comstock area. That she braved the hardships of a stage trip all the way from Sacramento over the Sierra Nevada Mountains was commendable," the article continued. She "was imbued with no-small share of courage and love of adventure which distinguished her husband…, and which finally carried him to his death in the Arctic regions.

She did not make the trip to Yosemite National Park in the expec-

The beautiful Vernal Falls from Lady Franklin Rock. COURTESY OF THE CALIFORNIA
HISTORY ROOM, CALIFORNIA STATE LIBRARY, SACRAMENTO, CALIFORNIA

tation of finding some old friend or acquaintance, but merely to satisfy her curiosity and gratify a desire she felt to visit a spot in which thousands of adventurers flocked from all parts of the world.[18]

Notice of Lady Franklin's arrival had originally been published in the Virginia City, Nevada, newspaper the *Territorial Enterprise*, "and all in the town felt honored by the visits of a personage so widely known and distinguished," the article noted. "Though all in the camp felt that nothing was too good for Lady Franklin, and though she commanded the sympathy and admiration of every one, yet not a man or woman intruded upon her presence even though there was a great demand to see her."[19]

From the Comstock area, Lady Franklin journeyed to Yosemite. She had to be carried to many scenic spots in the park because of her failing health. Once the touring party reached the area that Lady Franklin where had hired them to take her, they placed her frail, tired frame upon a broad, flat rock below Vernal Falls so she could admire the natural wonder. That spot has since become known as Lady Franklin Rock.[20]

Lady Jane Franklin returned to England, leaving San Francisco in late 1863. She died on July 18, 1875, of natural causes. According to the July 31, 1875, edition of the Perry, Iowa, newspaper *Perry Chief*, she "died poor in this world's goods by reason of her love for her husband and rich in the world's love and memory by virtue of her peerless heroism."

Lady Jane Franklin was eighty-three when she passed away.

Florence Hutchings

A Rebel Lost Too Soon

Fifteen-year-old Gertrude Hutchings sat on the edge of her sister Florence's bed, crying. Florence, a pretty girl of seventeen with long, dark hair lay motionless under a mountain of blankets. A massive purple and black bruise on the side of her right cheek was the only color on her slender, pale face. Her eyes were closed and her hands were folded across her chest, her breathing was labored and slow. Her grandmother, Florantha Sproat, dabbed the teenager's forehead with a cool, moist cloth, kissed her forehead, and then stepped away waiting for the girl to respond.[1]

Florence did not move. She would never move again. She died on September 26, 1881. Family and friends that surrounded her wept and wondered aloud to one another how someone so young and vibrant could be gone from them. "Yosemite Valley was diminished in a sense by her passing," one of Florence's teachers said at the young girl's funeral. "She was a rarity and added to the setting's beauty."[2]

Florence "Floy" Hutchings was the first white child born in Yosemite. Her parents, James Mason Hutchings, a businessman, farmer, and promoter of Yosemite National Park, and artist Elvira Sproat, welcomed their daughter into the world on August 24, 1864. The precocious, inquisitive child was the first child for the couple who lived in a log cabin close to Yosemite Falls.[3]

In addition to exploring the land that James Hutchings and John Muir would help preserve, James was a homesteader in the north section of Yosemite, where he raised fruit trees, strawberry plants, and various livestock, including horses. He also owned an inn that Florence's mother and he ran. Elvira was a reluctant innkeeper; she preferred painting, reading poetry, writing, and playing music. Her mother, Florantha, assumed the responsibility of caring for Floy and the two other children the Hutchings had: Gertrude, a blue-eyed, fair-haired girl born in October 1867, and William, a cheerful boy born in July 1869 who suffered from a spinal deformity.[4]

Despite her best efforts, Florantha had a difficult time raising Floy to be a proper young lady. Even as a small child she cared little for frilly dresses, curly hair, and ribbons. She was a tomboy and enjoyed collecting insects and toads, hiking, camping, and riding horses. She would often disappear for hours at a time to explore the valley and mountains. Although her mother would be furious with Floy for taking off without letting anyone know where she was going, the young girl refused to change and was seldom sorry for making her mother [and grandmother] worry.[5]

Naturalist John Muir, who worked for Floy's father, referred to Floy as "a smart, handsome, and mischievous Topsy that could scarce be overdrawn." It was not uncommon for the spirited Floy to jump on her horse and ride alongside the wagon trains or stage coaches traveling into the area to see the sights. Passengers would watch in amazement as the young girl boldly sped after the vehicles.[6]

Charles Warren Stoddard, a poet and musician from San Francisco, and frequent guest of the Hutchings family, wrote about the fearless Floy in his memoirs. "She is constant motion…lightening quick motion," he noted. "Dear little squirrel," a nickname given to her because of her fast, sudden moves, "she knew nothing of the world but what she saw of it within her mountain-walled horizon; such an odd little child she was, left to herself and her fancies; no doubt thinking she was the only one of

her kind in existence; contented to see-saw for hours on a plank by the woodpile; making long, solitary explanations, and returning, when we were all well frightened, with a pocket full of lizards and a wasp caged in her hand. They never stung her."[7]

Six-year-old Floy made an impression on a number of visitors to her parents' inn at Yosemite. In 1870 she enthusiastically introduced herself to an English novelist who memorialized the occasion in his journal. "Say! Listen!" he reported. Floy began a conversation after pinching him on his arm to gain his full attention. "Where do you come from; do you want to camp out? I'll go with you. We better start before the moon goes down; have you plenty of blankets? It's only twenty miles to the top of Tis-sa'-ak [Half Dome]. I'll show you the trail. I've just come down today. You are not afraid of rattlesnakes, I suppose; there is one just below here that has bitten me three times, but I always cut the piece out with my jack knife, and it did me no harm....Say! Do you want a polecat skin? I'll go out and catch and skin one alive, and bring it to you."[8]

Floy learned to read and write from her mother but had no formal education in her early years. She listened intently to the books Elvira read aloud and to the discussions the adults had with both her parents about politics, religion, and finances. According to John Muir's reminiscences, Floy frequently offered comments on a variety of subjects beyond the intelligence of some grownups.[9]

Neither Elvira nor James ever stifled their children's desire to ask questions or engage in conversation with adults. They were not, however, as permissive with their diet. Elvira was strict about the amount of food Floy, Gertrude, and William consumed and made them follow a regiment of eating mostly alfalfa, fruit, and some meat on special occasions. Water was the only beverage the children were allowed to drink. It wasn't uncommon for Floy and her siblings to visit John Muir at his cabin and beg for food. He always made sure the children got plenty of bread to eat and milk to drink when they called on him. After the three had their stomachs full, John would take them hiking and teach them about flowers and wildlife in the area. Recalling those times years later, Gertrude said that John Muir was "gracious and attentive to all of us."[10]

Jeanne Carr, one of John's closest friends, developed quite a fondness for the Hutchings children, particularly Floy. "I think with delight of how the winter home looks, of little brown 'squirrel' in the glow of the firelight," she wrote about the little girl in 1871.[11]

Keen interest in preserving the natural beauty of Yosemite brought about big changes in Floy's life and the lives of her family as a whole in 1874. Congress set aside the Yosemite Valley and the neighboring Mariposa Grove,and turned them over to the state of California to administer for all the people for all time. James Hutchings, along with a handful of other families who had been living in the region for a number of years, were forced to leave. Hutchings received $24,000 for the land he had worked as a homestead. Racing her horse over the rocky paths and through mountain passes of her childhood home would never be as easy for Floy again. The broken-hearted girl said goodbye to the beautiful, vast area that was once her playground and moved to San Francisco to live with her grandmother Florantha. The older woman had moved to the city several years prior to the family's having to leave Yosemite.[12]

Not long after the Hutchings relocated, Floy's parents' marriage began to fall apart. Elvira was not content to stay home with the children. She craved the excitement of attending art showings, going to the theatre, and meeting new and interesting people. She had an affair which led to the ultimate demise of the Hutchings' union. James and Elvira divorced in 1876.[13]

Florantha continued the day-to-day care of her grandchildren and managing the household. Floy and her siblings lived at Florantha's home the majority of the year and attended the local San Francisco school. During the summer months James would escort Floy back to Yosemite where she spent time hiking and riding her horse. Landscape painter Thomas Hill, photographer Edwin Muybridge, and botanist Albert Kellogg accompanied the Hutchings on their outdoor jaunts. Floy's spontaneity and love for the open spaces amused the talented individuals who traveled with James and his children. Floy's unladylike antics, such as riding astride and venturing off on her own, were the source of many conversations, and inspired all who knew her. "We all wished to be able to throw caution and tradition to the wind with such enthusiasm," Muybridge wrote in his memoirs.[14]

Just prior to her sixteenth birthday in 1880, Floy's father remarried. His new wife, the widow Augusta Sweetland, a landscape painter and newspaper correspondent, was not fond of Floy. And Floy didn't care for her either. Whether the reason that the pair didn't get along was jealousy or resentment is not entirely known. Perhaps it was Floy's refusal to conform to Augusta's idea of what a proper lady should be. Floy did struggle

Mount Florence, named for the feisty, daring young woman Florence Hutchings.
COURTESY OF YOSEMITE NATIONAL PARK LIBRARY

in school over the same issue. Teachers could not harness Floy's restless nature, and she didn't care to learn what books and administrators told her she had to learn. Floy was expelled from school at the same time her father was appointed guardian over Yosemite Park.[15]

Sixteen-year-old Floy returned with James to Yosemite. As soon as they reached their old homestead, she hurried off to the meadows and the mountains. A women's group exploring the wilderness hired her once as a guide. Floy happily introduced the inquisitive ladies to the high country's rarely traveled peaks and valleys. She educated them on the customs of the indigenous people and the habits of the animals that made Yosemite their home.[16]

Mount Florence, seen from Fork of Lyell Basin Camp. COURTESY OF YOSEMITE NPS LIBRARY

In the winter of 1880, Augusta Sweetland died. Although she was sorry for her father's loss, the sudden demise of James's second wife had little effect on Floy. Florantha continued to act as "homemaker, doctor, cook, spinner of yarn, knitter of stockings in our homes as long as she lived in Yosemite and San Francisco," Floy's sister Gertrude recalled many years later.[17]

Floy continued her routine of communing with nature and discovering Yosemite's hidden treasures. One of her most favorite places was the old chapel located on the south side of the Merced River. It had a seating capacity of one hundred persons. The tiny, New England–style church was built under sponsorship of the California State Sunday School Children. The original reed organ was a gift from Miss Mary Porter of Philadelphia in memory of Floy.[18]

Floy's contagiously vivacious personality was the inspiration for the title character in a novel written by Theresa Yelverston, entitled *Zanita: A Tale of the Yosemite*. Yelverston, a controversial woman from Britain, was more than a little preoccupied with naturalist John Muir, his time in Yosemite, and the people he knew—Floy Hutchings being one of them. She believed Floy had the talent to become a great actress. Yelverston wanted to adopt the girl and personally train her for a stage career. Not only would Floy's father not allow it, but Floy had no interest in ever leaving Yosemite again.[19]

Floy had a deep affection for other children who resided in her beloved Yosemite. She always took time out of her daily horseback rides to stop and visit with them and play a few games. Oftentimes her best friend, Effie Crippen, daughter of former Maricopa County Sheriff Joshua Crippen, would join her on visits with the children. Effie had grown up in the Valley with Floy. The two also hiked and climbed rocks together. Effie died in 1881 from a cut she received on a broken bottle. She was wading in Mirror Lake when she stepped on a piece of glass on the floor of the lake. It severed an artery and she bled to death.[20]

Not long after Effie passed away, Floy took a job working as a caretaker for the Yosemite Chapel located near Half Dome. Her duties included dusting, sweeping, decorating, and, on occasion, ringing the church bell for the services.[21]

On September 11, 1874, Floy wrote a poem that expressed her gratitude for being able to live and work in the Yosemite Valley. "Beautiful.

Wonderful. How come you are? For what has nature caused this awe inspiring deep canon and high towering peaks from it is to remind one there is a God, and that his works are the works of nature? That His works are wonderful beyond comprehension." The moving verses are included in a compilation of other thoughts about the scenic area written by thousands of visitors on file at the Yosemite Museum.[22]

In early fall 1881, Floy succumbed to the injuries she sustained in a tragic hiking accident. She died just three weeks after the passing of her best friend. "A party of friends were climbing the ledge trail when someone above her accidentally loosened a large rock and it rolled down, striking Florence," Gertrude Hutchings recalled in her memoirs in 1949. "She died the following day." Ironically, Floy's death mirrored the death of the character patterned after her in the novel Theresa Yelverston wrote. "She had missed her footing and pitched headlong over the brow of Tis-sa-ack [Half Dome]," Yelverston penned in her book *Zanita: A Tale of the Yosemite*. "The piece of her dress hanging on the bushes denotes she has fallen...."[23]

Florence "Floy" Hutchings' funeral was held at the hotel her father, mother, and grandmother operated when she was a child. A family member offered a few words about Floy's shocking passing. Her sentiments echoed the thoughts of many at the service. "Only a week before she was climbing heights and scrambling through ravines where eagles might be looked for...."[24]

Among the many people who attended her service were artists C.D. Robinson, Charles Dorman Taylor, and author and poet Benjamin F. Taylor. Not long after Floy's death, Charles Dorman Taylor asked the National Park Committee to consider naming a mountain in Yosemite to honor the feisty teenager. A 12,561-foot peak west of Mount Lyell, as well as a nearby lake, were named after the adventurous young woman.[25]

Clare Hodges

First Female Ranger in the Nation

Twenty-seven-year-old Clare Hodges gently urged her chestnut roan through a thicket of trees and brush. The horse's hooves barely made a sound as it walked over a thick carpet of pine needles and maple leaves. Bright streams of sunlight filtered through the branches of sequoias and spilled onto the ground with brilliant intensity. A light breeze escorted horse and rider and deposited them at the edge of a massive emerald meadow. Jagged lofty peaks waited on the other side of the grassy area, and above it all was a cloudless, deep blue sky, verging on the color of indigo.[1]

Clare surveyed Yosemite National Park's Kings River Canyon carefully. A park ranger for all of two months, she was patrolling the spectacular setting, just part of her job since signing on with the National Park Service in late spring 1918. An article in the June 1, 1919, issue of the *Lima* [Ohio] *News*, reported that Clare's love for the mountains prompted her to pursue a profession as a park ranger and that "the beauty of the region made the work a pleasure."

One of the many duties Clare had as a park ranger was to routinely scrutinize the bold peak of Mount Hutchings (a 10,758-foot peak overlooking Kings River Canyon) for rock climbers in trouble, and the floor below for hikers who had lost their way. She never encountered anyone in such a dire predicament. As she studied the vast area "the spray from the fifty foot waterfall over the steep mountain would fall on my face," Clare recalled later in her life. "The water made a beautiful fan of foam that spread out in a turbulent, eddying mass into the roaring river below."[2] Apart from mule deer, eagles, a few cougars, curious chipmunks, and wolves, Clare rarely encountered any living inhabitants in her daily routine. "My life as a ranger is not as wild and woolly as it sounds," she told the *Lima News*.

From May 22 to September 7, 1918, Clare was the only female mountain ranger in the United States. Her responsibilities were the same as those of her male counterparts. She answered telephone calls, registered tourists, assigned campsites, issued auto permits, made reports, confiscated firearms, hiked to camp grounds, noted conditions of the campsites, counted campers, and patrolled Yosemite National Park. "The Valley," she explained to *Sunset* magazine for its February 1919 issue, "became like an open book to me...."

Clare Marie Hodges was born on December 1, 1890, in Branciforte, Santa Cruz County, California. She made her first horseback trip to Yosemite with her parents John and Mary Hodges when she was thirteen years old. The four-day journey was one of the most influential times in her life. She learned a great deal about the land and its history en route to the park. Her father taught her about Yosemite's rock formations, the wildlife that lived there, and the types of flowers and plants that existed at various mountain elevations. Clare learned that those who had swarmed into California in search of gold in 1849 soon discovered there were other wonderful things there as well—Yosemite being one of them.[3]

In 1864 Congress set aside the Yosemite Valley and the neighboring Mariposa Grove of big trees and turned them over to the state of California to administer. In 1890, coincidentally the year Clare was born, the area became a national park. "I learned to love the mountains," Clare

From atop her horse, Clare Hodges surveys the Yosemite Valley to make sure that all is well. COURTESY OF YOSEMITE NPS LIBRARY

confessed to a reporter with the *Fresno Bee* in November 1963. "In 1913 I rode to Tuolumne Meadows, and I returned five or six times a year after that."

It wasn't until 1916 that Clare decided periodic trips to Yosemite wouldn't suffice. She wanted to live there. By then Clare had graduated from high school and attended college. She became a school teacher and relocated from San Jose to Mariposa County to take a job with the Yosemite School. In the *Sunset* interview, she explained that her pupils were mostly the children of rangers, other government employees, and Indian residents. "I grew very fond of my aboriginal charges and they taught me something of woodcraft in exchange for what they learned of a white man's lore," she noted. The school district where Clare worked had been established in 1875 by another pioneer in the region, inn keeper Isabella Leidig and her husband George Leidig.[4]

In addition to teaching school and caring for her family, Clare wrote poetry. Inspired by her daily surroundings, she penned a number of poems about the area. Clare had developed an interest in poetry at a very young age, and after a trip to Yosemite in 1913 she wrote a poem about the journey entitled "The Land of Wandering." It was originally published in the *Pacific Short Story Club Magazine* in 1914.

> O, the mountains call and I feel their thrall,
> And into the saddle I swing,
> For keenest love 'neath heaven above
> Is the love of wandering.
> Where the grey cliffs rise to the blue of the skies,
> And freedom and rest they bring,
> Past the sparkling lake where ripples break
> Lies the Path of the Wandering.[5]

A dramatic change in Clare's life, as well as the lives of all Americans, took place on April 6, 1917. That was the day the United States officially joined World War I. By the summer of 1918 more than two million men had been called to serve. Jobs traditionally held by men were left vacant, or women were hired to fill those open positions. Clare saw a need for park rangers and decided to find out if she could apply for one of the empty posts. "Probably you'll laugh at me," she told W.B. Lewis, supervisor of the Yosemite Park District, "but I want to be a ranger." "I beat you to it, young lady," Wilson told her. "It's been on my mind for some time to put a woman on one of these patrols, only I couldn't find the right one before."[6]

Lewis submitted Clare's application to Washington, and within a month all was approved and she was given a badge, uniform, and a horse. According to the interview Clare did with *Sunset* magazine, it was as if all the years she'd spent exploring Yosemite's mountains and valleys had led to that moment. Clare reported directly to the chief ranger from the time she took on the job until she relinquished the position back to the men she replaced. Lewis bragged to magazine and newspaper reporters that Clare performed her job with "fearless dexterity and efficiency."[7]

Clare patrolled all over Yosemite, from the base of Nevada Falls (close to the Merced River) along the Wawona Road (near the Mariposa Grove) to Half Dome high above the valley floor on Glacier Point. "It was such an adventure," she told the writer for *Sunset*. "Once, with a ranger friend, we made our way under a frozen waterfall and in an ice cap cooked our luncheon of bacon and eggs," Clare continued, referring to the experience. "It was quite a feather in my cap because they told us no woman would dare attempt it."[8]

The uniform Clare wore was a khaki ensemble consisting of a shirt, gaucho pants, ranger hat, and leather gauntlets. The entire outfit was called "camping clothes." The badge affixed to the right breast pocket of her shirt was labeled with her park service affiliation number, which was [npshpc – hfc/yose] #931.[9] Fellow rangers strongly suggested that Clare carry a gun, in case someone tried to rob her of the park funds she guarded, but she refused. "I carried money (gate receipts) from Tuolumne Meadows the park headquarters," she told the *Fresno Bee* staff writer. "It was an overnight ride in those days, but I never had any trouble along the way."

Throughout the summer of 1918 many journalists visited Yosemite in search of the lone woman government forest ranger in Yosemite. They wanted to know what it was like to work in such a "breathtakingly beautiful spot." An article in the August 26, 1918, edition of the Massachusetts newspaper the *Lowell Sun* depicted her daily duties in this way: "She has nothing to do except wear her khaki riding habit and lope all day through the forest aisles, over lily-decked meadows, past thundering waterfalls, along foaming torrents, and ledge trails overlooking dizzy cliffs, with a glittering chain of snowy peaks in the background."

By late 1918, Clare's employment with the park service was terminated. Soldiers who had once been park rangers returned from the war and were eager to have their jobs back. There wouldn't be another woman hired as a ranger until 1923.[10]

Clare returned to the Bay Area where she taught school and became the president of the literary society of the San Jose Normal School. It was during this time that she met and married Earl Seiverson. Seiverson was a clerk at a mercantile. The news of their nuptials was posted in the November 2, 1918, edition of the *Mariposa Gazette*. "Miss Clare Hodges...was married in Stockton on October 19, 1918, to Earl Lester

Seiverson. The couple spent a few days in Mariposa the latter part of last week." The couple divorced shortly after the birth of their son, Forest Glen, on June 24, 1920.[11]

In 1927 Clare married poultry farmer Peter Wolfsen. The pair resided in Cathey's Valley, California, an area known for some of the richest grazing land in the state. Clare and her husband were very involved with activities at their church. She worked with children at the church summer camp program in Yosemite for more than thirty-five years, teaching them how to ride a horse and how to identify flowers and trees. She was often called upon by the staff of the San Jose State College to deliver lectures on wildflowers and herbarium. Clare and Peter enjoyed gathering seeds along Sierra trails to renew wildflower gardens around Northern California. A nature trail in Merced County was named for the Wolfsens.[12]

Peter died on July 29, 1958, after suffering with a bout of pneumonia. He was ninety-one years old. Clare and Peter had been married for more than thirty years when he passed away.[13]

Clare married for a third time in 1963. Ernest Morris shared her love of Yosemite and agreed to honeymoon at the national park. "We made the trip from Cathey's Valley with a trailer," Clare shared with the *Fresno Bee* in February 1963. "I prefer horses to automobiles. They're less tiresome."[14]

At the age of seventy-three, Clare still enjoyed riding through Yosemite Park on the backs of her favorite horse. The grassy meadows, towering cliffs, tumultuous rivers, cascading waterfalls, and incredible chasms continued to inspire her to write poems about the region.[15] A poem Clare penned entitled "Tuolumne" described her affection for the eastern section of Yosemite National Park.

> How often in my dreams I see
> Thy mountains beckon luringly,
> Thy granite spires, Tuolumne,
> Cathedral Peaks and Lambert Dome,
> The wide-winged eagle's rugged home.
> Thy great grey crags where cloudlets rest,

And rising calm above thy breast
The summits of thy hoary crest;
Each dear spot in my memory
So soft recall, Tuolumne.
I see thee in the morning sheen,
Thy river calm its banks between,
Thy shimmering robe of meadow green,
Thy sparkling dew on blade and tree,
Thy jeweled veil, Tuolumne.
Each dimple holds a glittering lake,
Where mirrored forest shadows break,
And gentle breezes ripple wake,
Thy sparkling streams in gayiety
Are girdling gems, Tuolumne.[16]

Clare Hodges died on June 20, 1970, in Loma Linda University Medical Center, San Bernardino, California. She was cremated, and her ashes were placed on her husband's casket. Clare was eighty years old.[17]

Erin Sugako Davenport
& Julia Florence Parker
Archaeologist and Basket Weaver

Compliance Specialist and archaeologist Erin Sugako Davenport sat alone near the top of Nevada Falls in Yosemite National Park admiring a commanding view of the valley floor nearly two hundred feet below. The landmark Liberty Cap and Half Dome competed for her attention. It was four in the morning. She had hiked from Glacier Point in the middle of the night so she could be the first person to summit Half Dome the following day. A glorious sunrise promised to bathe the granite, forests, and waterfalls before her, in gold and pine. Although the sight was not new to her it never failed to inspire.

Yosemite has been referred to as the great outdoor cathedral and that only the most hardened could fail to feel the sublimity of the national park. As an employee, Erin is dedicated to preserving the integrity of the spectacular setting for all who venture west to experience the sublimity themselves.[1]

While reflecting on the thousands of visitors that have been to Yosemite and those yet to come, Erin noticed a pair of glowing eyes peering out from a copse of trees in the near distance. At first she thought it might be a deer, but upon closer inspection she realized the eyes belonged to a

Basket weaver Julia Parker demonstrates her skill for Yosemite visitors.
COURTESY OF YOSEMITE NPS LIBRARY

Yosemite National Park compliance specialist Erin Davenport scales mountains in Yosemite and elsewhere.
COURTESY OF ERIN DAVENPORT

mountain lion. In an area abundant with wildlife from sleek, sluggish, black bears to striped chipmunks, it wasn't unusual to see animals roaming around. The square-faced mountain lion was too busy drinking water from a small creek across the trail to take much notice of Erin. She watched the animal quench his thirst and eventually wander off. Erin waited for the sun to start its ascent in the sky before continuing on her way.[2]

Erin had by then worked for the park service for more than twelve years, and happily admitted that there's an exciting story associated with every month she's been on the job. "I work full time as a compliance specialist," Erin proudly offered. "My job gives me the opportunity to not only get the gist of the inner workings of park planning efforts, but I also get to use my expertise as an archaeologist–cultural resources subject matter specialist."

Born in 1976, Erin began visiting Yosemite when she was two years old. She came of age at a memorable retreat celebrating her twelfth birthday at Crane Flat, and received her first kiss in the Curry Village cabins. The influence the beautiful region had on her prompted her to pursue a degree in conservation and resource studies from U.C. Berkeley. In 1999, she began teaching outdoor education in the Santa Cruz Mountains. By the year 2000 she had embarked on basket weaving, training with accomplished craftswoman Julia Parker. "Julia had a great impact on my life," Erin noted.

Julia Florence Parker was a forty-year employee at Yosemite. She was an expert weaver who learned the craft from some of the leading twentieth century indigenous California basket weavers. At the age of nineteen, Julia married into a Yosemite Indian tribe and studied the art of baskets from her mother-in-law, expert Lucy Telles. Julia and Julia's daughter passed on her skills to Erin. Julia is both the oldest and longest-serving park employee. Like her mentor, Erin used the skills she had learned to create one-of-a-kind baskets and treasure boxes.[3]

American writer and political activist Jesse Benton Fremont is another of Erin's heroes. Jesse led the crusade to keep Yosemite safe from eager land developers bent on altering the region. "She was ahead of her time in California for having an eye for the environment and preserving the beautiful place," Erin passionately stated. "If not for her efforts I might not be working here today."

In 2001 Erin took a teaching position, and taught outdoor education at the Yosemite Institute. The tragic murder of a popular teacher named Joie Armstrong who worked at the institute had occurred a few years before Erin took the job. Joie's life was cut short by serial killer Cary Stayner in 1999.

> The community was in mourning. When I started work, I inherited all of Joie's teaching materials. That meant a great deal to me. Her strong spirit will always be important to women who work at the Yosemite Institute. The strength of the person she was, and the incredible community of friends

and family who gathered strength, creativity, and kinship in the wake of her death have had a profound effect on how women in Yosemite embrace the beauty, comfort, and challenges of this landscape.

Erin was officially hired as an archaeologist with the National Park Service in 2004. She studied artifacts and the people who used them. "Some of the finds made at Yosemite date back ten thousand years," Erin said. Erin, along with several other seasoned professionals, studied only objects found at the park that are more than fifty years old. Objects that may not seem like much to the layman have great significance to the archaeologists at Yosemite. According to an article about the National Park Service printed in the *Washington Post*, "cans found at a construction camp can indicate the number of workers and the length of stay at a particular camp. Chinese ceramics and imported food containers in refuse piles along the river reveal information about trade networks and the ethnic groups that were living and working in the park hundreds of years ago."[4]

In 2006 Erin decided to enroll in the master's program at Sonoma State. Her focus was on cultural resources management, defined as the practice managing cultural resources such as arts and heritage. She achieved her goal while maintaining her regular park work schedule. Upon graduating she became a compliance specialist on the Half Dome Stewardship Plan, a proposal to better maintain the hiking trails on and around the mountain, to better protect the area's natural and cultural resources, and to better protect the wilderness, support the Merced River Plan (a proposal to designate and mark river access points), to protect the wildlife and the scenic river corridor, and to support the American Indian Liaison Program. That last is a plan to ensure that the park collaborates with traditionally-associated American Indian tribes and groups when making decisions that could affect resources or access to resources of traditional, or other cultural significance. Erin believes that such programs are necessary because "the integrity of the park must be sustained." "There are approximately three million visitors to Yosemite a year," she reported. "We are in danger of loving the place to death."

Like other pioneering women who have lived and worked at Yosemite National Park, Erin finds her job to be "extremely rewarding."

I've thoroughly enjoyed everything I've been able to do at the park, from working at the Yosemite Institute educating youth about the region to escorting tours through the sequoia groves.

Her favorite spot in Yosemite is Big Meadow. It is composed of hundreds of acres of grassland surrounded by hills that cradle the peaceful meadow.

There's a lot of history here. A long history of people who loved the area whose presence can still be felt, people pounding rocks with pestles, holding hands with their children and singing songs.

It's where I had my wedding reception in 2006. I chose to have my wedding there because the sunsets and sunrises are so spectacular. But it's the full moon nights in Big Meadow that I love the most. A giant harvest moon rose over the meadow the night of the wedding. It's everyone's best memory from the night."

Throughout the course of her National Park Service career, Erin has scaled the granite rocks of Yosemite's most picturesque peaks, including Tenaya Peak and Mount Conness.

I've been climbing for years. I got my first rock climbing harness, shoes, and rope in 1999.

Erin enjoys rock climbing because it takes her to beautiful places in an intimate group. "Intimacy is what builds relationships," she said, "whether it is with people or a landscape."

Signs from wildfires that ran across parts of Yosemite in 1991 and 2009 can still be seen by trained eyes like Erin's, but she is quick to point out that "nature is resilient with amazing recuperative powers."

In 2010, Erin and her husband, Andrew, a Yosemite fire fighter, welcomed a son into their lives. Erin enjoys seeing the splendor of the park through his young eyes.

He's so excited to see a bear in a tree or a deer or two wandering by. I am convinced that Yosemite is the best place for me to live, work, and raise my boy. The unpredictable mountain life with all of its rock falls, fires, floods, snowstorms, et cetera really suits me.

When asked about the future for women with the National Park Service in Yosemite, Erin noted that the various skills and talents female rangers, environmentalists, Indian liaisons, tour guides, and fire fighters have to offer will always be in demand. "Women who have devoted their entire lives to serving the park are an inspiration to me," she said. "And dedicated women in this park will continue to move mountains."

Among the women Erin listed as those she admired was Julia Florence Parker, a Coast Miwok–Kashaya Pomo Indian basket weaver and

Diagram 1

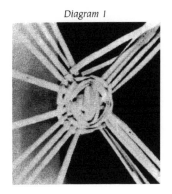

Diagram 2

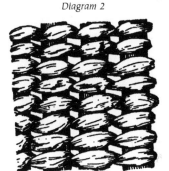

Diagram 4
Left: One-rod coiling.
Right: Three-rod coiling.

Diagram 3

the recognized authority on California Indian culture. Born in 1928, she studied with some of the 20th century's leading indigenous California basket weavers. By the age of eighty-four, she had become one of the preeminent Native American basket makers in California.[5]

Many different native plants are utilized as material by Yosemite Indian women like Julia to make baskets. Willow, squaw bush, red-bud (a shrub or tree native to the dry inner coastal range), tule-root, maidenhair fern, brake fern, wire bunch grass and the red strips of bark from the creek dogwood are a few of the most commonly items used.

Several types of twining techniques are used to construct the baskets. Twining, as shown in diagrams #1 and #2, provides the basket with a heavy base. Twine baskets were primarily used for carrying heavy loads. Coiling, as shown in diagrams #3 and #4, was used in making ceremonial baskets.

Each basket is designed with a specific purpose in mind. Mush-bowl baskets—small, closely-woven works—are used for serving foods. Dipper baskets are small, tightly woven baskets used for holding liquids. Cradles, of openwork basketry, or "hickey" as the Yosemite Indians refer to them, are woven and then covered with deer skin for carrying a child.[6]

Afterword
by
Beth Rodden, World-Renowned Rock Climber

Yosemite holds an extraordinary place is so many people's hearts. From the single-day traveler driving through, to the people who call Yosemite home, its magnificent landscape sears its way into anyone's memory.

I have called Yosemite home for the past seven years, finally putting down roots after living out of my car in the park for almost fifteen years. As a professional rock climber, I was originally drawn to Yosemite for its grand granite walls and world renowned climbing. Recently, however, the majestic scenery of Yosemite has drawn me even deeper to explore all parts of the park.

Numerous stories are told of the men who discovered and developed the park, but few are told of the women. This book does an exemplary job of highlighting some of the incredible women who added to the rich fabric of Yosemite's history. As a woman, I continually draw strength and inspiration from others who paved the way for the next generation.

I recently had an outing up Mount Starr King, just south of Half Dome. While small in comparison to some of the highest rock faces or peaks in Yosemite, the relative remoteness is special for its proximity to the road. After several hours on the trail, we arrived at the awe-inspiring summit, with 360-degree views of the valley and the high Sierra. Dutifully I signed the summit register and read about the people who had stood on the same glorious summit. To my surprise, many of the people before us were women, from a few days prior to a decade prior. In the past decade, I have noticed an almost equal amount of women climbing and exploring the vast national park, a true testament to those early female pioneers.

Women such as Sally Dutcher and Elizabeth Pershing climbed beside men on some of the first summittings in Yosemite, setting the tone that women could also pioneer and explore. Nowadays, women are not only climbing beside, but also ahead of their, male counterparts. One of my heroes, Lynn Hill, paved the way for all climbers, men and women, with her legendary first free ascent of The Nose of El Capitan in the early 1990s. Without her vision and perseverance, the most famous rock climb in the world would have not been free climbed for at least a decade. I was on the team to make the coveted second ascent of The Nose, and at every difficult point I thought of Lynn's ascent. As I climb or hike throughout the park, I constantly think of the women who came before me, who planted the seed of curiosity deep inside me.

All the women in this book were instrumental in making Yosemite what it is today. Without early pioneers like these, we might not have had Yosemite as a protected area along with the rich history of caring and exploring in the park. Women have been instrumental all along the way. I know that, with the continuing influence of women like Erin Sugako Davenport, we will all play leading roles in Yosemite's future, carving out a place for generations of women to come.

Bibliography

Books

Bingaman, John W. *Guardians of the Yosemite: A Story of the First Rangers.* Yosemite: Literary Licensing, Yosemite National Park Service, 1961.

Birge, Julius. *Awakening in the Desert.* Boston: Richard Badger Books, 1912.

Denton, Sally. *Passion & Principle: John & Jessie Fremont, the Couple Whose Power, Politics, & Love Shaped Nineteenth-Century America.* Lincoln: University of Nebraska Press, 2007.

Fremont, Jessie B. *Far-West Sketches.* Boston: D. Lothrop Company, 1890.

Godfrey, Elizabeth. Yosemite Indians. Yosemite: Yosemite Natural History Association, 1973.

Herr, Pamela. *Jessie Benton Fremont.* Norman: University of Oklahoma Press, 1988.

Haight, Sarah. *Diary of Sarah Haight.* San Francisco: The Grabhorn Press, 1858.

Hutchings, James. *In the Heart of the Sierra.* Paris, France: Ulan Press, 1886.

Miller, Sally M., and Daryl Morrison. *John Muir: Family, Friends & Adventure.* Albuquerque: University of New Mexico Press, 2005.

Muir, John, and William Bade. *The Life and Letters of John Muir* Vol. 2. Boston: Houghton Mifflin Company, 1924.

Palmquist, Peter E. *Carleton Watkins: Photographer of the North American West.* Albuquerque: University of New Mexico, 1983.

Risjord, Norman. *Representative Americans: Populists & Progressives.* Lanham,

MD: Rowman & Littlefield Publishers, 2005.

Russell, Carl P. *One Hundred Years in Yosemite: The Story of a Great Park and Its Friends*. Berkeley: University of California Press, 1947.

Sanborn, Margaret. *Yosemite: Its Discovery, Its Wonders & Its People*. New York: Random House, 1981.

Sargent, Shirley. *Pioneers in Petticoats*. Los Angeles: Trans-Anglo Books, 1966.

Sargent, Shirley. *Yosemite: A National Treasure*. Yosemite: Yosemite Park & Curry Company, 1992.

Sargent, Shirley. *Galen Clark: Yosemite Guardian*. Yosemite: Flying Spur Press, 1981.

Sargent, Shirley. *Yosemite Inn Keepers*. Yosemite: Flying Spur Press, 1975.

Secrest, William. *The Great Yosemite Holdups*. Fresno, CA: Saga-West Publishing, 1973.

Yelverston, Theresa. *Zanita: A Tale of the Yosemite*. New York: Hurd & Houghton, 1872.

Worster, Donald. *A Passion for Nature: The Life of John Muir*. Stockton, CA: University of the Pacific, 1997.

Interviews
Email interviews with Erin Davenport. October 23, 2012 & November 26, 2012; phone interview with Erin Davenport, October 25, 2012.

Websites
www.ancestry.com
www.caeducation.com
www.californiabaskets.com
www.cdn.calisphere.org/muirletters
www.findagrave.com/GeorgeLeidig
www.thehive.modbee.com
www.legendarylearningnow.com/johnmuir
www.martinez.patch.com
www.nls.uk.franklin
www.nps.gov/
www.sierraclub.org/
www.stanford.education/
www.undiscoveredyosemite.com/FlorenceHutchings
www.worthpoint.com
www.yosemite.ca.us/library/
www.yosemiteexperience.com
www.yosemitenews.info/forum.com

Periodicals

Anderson, Ralph. "Ta-bu-ce." *Yosemite Nature Notes* XXVI, No. 7 (July 1947).

Berkovitch, Ellen. "Photog Carleton Watkins Blazed New Trails." *The New Mexican Magazine* 28 (March 28-April 6, 2000).

Degnan, Laurence V. "The Yosemite Valley School." *Yosemite Nature Notes,* XXXV No. 2 (February 1956).

Johnston, Hank. "Yosemite's Pioneer Lower Hotel." *Yosemite: A Journal for Members of the Yosemite Association* 68, No. 1 (Winter 2006).

Matthews, Francois. "The Last Yosemite Highway Robbery." *Yosemite Nature Notes* XXVI, No. 12 (December 1947).

Kaufman, Polly W. "Pioneer Woman Naturalist in the National Park Service." *Forest & Conservation History* (January 1990).

Muir, John. "Treasures of Yosemite." *The Century Magazine* XL, No. 4 (August 1890).

Pacific Short Story Club Magazine 1-3, 7-10 (1914)

Payne Ernest. "Ta-bu-ce as a Weather Prophetess." *Yosemite Nature Notes* XVII, No. 2 (February 1938).

Pershing, Elizabeth. "A Trip to the Geyser." *National Repository Journal* 1 (April 1877).

Sharsmith, Carl W. "A Visit with Ta-bu-ce." *Yosemite Nature Notes* XXV No. 11 (November 1946).

Them Were the Days Magazine Fall 1996

Young, Robert W. "Ladies Who Wear the Uniform of the National Park Service." *Planning & Civil Comment* 28 No. 1 (March 1962).

Endnotes

Introduction

1. Nelson B. Keys, *The Real Book About Our National Parks* (New York: Doubleday & Co., Inc., 1957), 36-38.
2. Shirley Sargent, *Yosemite: A National Treasure* (Yosemite: Yosemite Park & Curry Company, 1992), 34-42.
3. Russell, Carl P. *One Hundred Years in Yosemite: The Story of a Great Park and Its Friends* (Berkeley: University of California Press, 1947), 5, 6-8.
4. The legend of Half Dome and Washington Tower is from *Oakland Tribune*, May 11, 1919.
5. *Cedar Rapids Gazette*, September 8, 1983.
6. Shirley Sargent, *Pioneers in Petticoats* (Los Angeles: Trans-Anglo Books, 1966), 41.
9. Ibid., 25-26; http://www.nps.gov/yose/parkmgmt/upload/12.08%20 Women-Adobe-7.pdf; www.stanford.edu/halfdome/.
10. William B. Secrest, *The Great Yosemite Holdups* (Fresno, CA: Saga-West Publishing, 1973), 13-17; Francois Matthes, "The Last Yosemite Highway Robbery," *Yosemite Nature Notes* XXVI:12 (December 1947).

Jessie Benton Fremont: Guardian of Yosemite

1. Knave column, *Oakland Tribune*, January 30, 1949; Margaret Sanborn, *Yosemite: Its Discovery, Its Wonders, & Its People* (New York: Random House, 1981), 86.
2. Pamela Herr, *Jessie Benton Fremont* (Norman: University of Oklahoma Press, 1988), 79.
3. Ibid., 163; *The Argus* (Melbourne, Australia), January 1, 1969.
4. Knave column.
5. Herr, 9-12.
6. Ibid., 63.
7. *Carroll Sentinel* (Carroll, IA), January 5, 1903.
8. *Washington Post*, May 24, 1914.
9. Jessie B. Fremont, *Far-West Sketches* (Boston: D. Lathrop Company, 1890), 78-82.

10. *Washington Post.*
11. *The Argus*; *Titusville Morning Herald* (Titusville,PA), September 27, 1880.
12. Fremont, 38-39; Herr, 193-196.
13. Herr, 192-194; Sanborn, 131.
14. Fremont, 42-50, 86-89.
15. Herr, 216-219.
16. Ibid., 221-225.
17. Ibid., 303-305.
18. *The Argus*, January 1, 1969; Herr, 280-283.
19. Sally Denton, *Passion & Principle: John & Jessie Fremont, the Couple Whose Power, Politics, & Love Shaped Nineteenth-Century America* (Lincoln: University of Nebraska Press, 2007), 280-283.
20. Sanborn, 99.
21. Fremont, 197-200.
22. Denton, 290-292.
23. Fremont, 399.
24. *Carroll Sentinel* (Carroll, IA), January 5, 1903; Fremont, 424.
25. Quoted in Nelson B. Keyes, *The Real Book About Our National Parks* (New York: Doubleday & Co., Inc., 1957), 36-38.

Anne Ripley, Elizabeth Fry, & Sara Haight: Weddings and Honeymoons

1. *Emporia Weekly Gazette* (Emporia, KS), May 2, 1902; Shirley Sargent, *Pioneers in Petticoats* (Los Angeles: Trans-Anglo Books Los Angeles, 1966), 51-52.
2. Quotations about the Ripley-Best wedding are from *Boston Globe*, August 6, 1901.
3. *The Daily Review* (Hayward, CA), August 1, 1965.
4. Quotations about the Ralston wedding trip are from Sarah Haight, *Diary of Sarah Haight* (San Francisco: The Grabhorn Press, 1858), 1-5.
5. *The Daily Review.*
6. *Janesville Daily Gazette* (Janesville, WI), September 9, 1915.

Elizabeth Pershing: Adventurous Journalist

1. *San Francisco Bulletin*, June 26, 1874; www.sierraclub.org/southdome.
2. *The Daily Sentinel* (Milwaukee, WI), July 24, 1860; Carl P. Russell, *One Hundred Years in Yosemite: The Story of a Great Park and Its Friends* (Berkeley: University of California Press, 1947).
3. John Muir, "Treasures of Yosemite," *The Century* XL:4 (August 1890); Margaret Sanborn, *Yosemite: Its Discovery, Its Wonders, & Its People* (New York: Random House, 1981), 78-79.
4. *Cincinnati Commercial*, October 18, 1876, accessed at http://www.stanford.

edu/~galic/history/halfdome/lizzie_pershing_letter.html/.
5. Ibid.; *Titusville Morning Herald* (Titusville, PA), September 13, 1876.
6. *San Francisco Bulletin*, June 26, 1876; *Cincinnati Commercial.*
7. *Louisville Courier*, November 12, 1876, accessed at www.ancestry.com/.
8. Sanborn, 78-79; www.sierraclub.org/southdome/.
9. Pershing's entire account of the climb is quoted from *Cincinnati Commercial,* October 18, 1876.
10. James Hutchings, *In the Heart of the Sierras* (n.p., Paris, France, 1886), 156-157.
11. www.ancestry.com/.

Isabella Logan Leidig: Self-Sufficient Innkeeper
1. Carl P. Russell, *One Hundred Years in Yosemite: The Story of a Great Park and Its Friends* (Berkeley: University of California Press, 1947), 102.
2. Shirley Sargent, *Pioneers in Petticoats* (Los Angeles: Trans-Anglo Books Los Angeles, 1966), 22.
3. Russell, 102.
4. www.findagrave.com/GeorgeLeidig; www.ancestry.com/; www.nps.gov/ IsabellaLeidig/.
5. Sargent, 21-23.
6. Ibid.
7. Shirley Sargent, *Galen Clark: Yosemite Guardian* (Yosemite: Flying Spur Press, 1981), 42-46.
8. Hank Johnston, "Yosemite's Pioneer Lower Hotel," *Yosemite: A Journal for Members of the Yosemite Association*, 68: 1 (Winter 2006), 5-7.
9. *Mariposa Gazette* (Mariposa, CA), July 20, 1871.
10. Margaret Sanborn, *Yosemite: Its Discovery, Its Wonders, & Its People* (New York: Random House, 1981), 89-91.
11. Sargent, *Yosemite Inn Keepers* (Yosemite: Flying Spur Press, 1975), 13-15.
12. Johnston.
13. *Mariposa Gazette*, June 8, 1867.
14. Sargent, *Pioneers in Petticoats,* 21.
15. Russell, 101-102.
16. Ibid., 89.
17. www.yosemite.ca.us/library/big_oak_flat_road.yosemite/.
18. Ibid.
19. Johnston.
20. www.findagrave.com/GeorgeLeidig; www.ancestry.com/; *Hayward Daily Review* (Hayward, CA), October 12, 1930.
21. *Hayward Daily Review.*
22. Ibid.

Maggie Howard: Paiute Basket Maker and Teacher
1. http://www.worthpoint.com/worthopedia/rppc-yosemites-ta-bu-ce-maggie-howard-172556535/.
2. Ibid.; "Yosemite Indian Cemetery; May Tom and Her Death," http://yosemitenews.info/forum/read.php?3,40433,40438/.
3. Ibid.
4. *Yosemite Nature Notes* XXVI:7 (July 1947), 83-88.
5. Shirley Sargent, *Pioneers in Petticoats* (Los Angeles: Trans-Anglo Books Los Angeles, 1966), 13-14.
6. Elizabeth Godfrey, *Yosemite Indians* (Yosemite: Yosemite Natural History Association, 1973), 12-14; *Yosemite Nature Notes* XXV:11 (November 1946), 127-129.
7. Godfrey, 18-19; *Yosemite Nature Notes* XVII:2 (February 1938), 37-38.
8. Ibid.
9. Sargent, *Pioneers in Petticoats*, 12-14.
10. *Yosemite Nature Notes* XXVI: 7 (July 1947), 83-88.
11. *Nevada State Journal* February 2, 1947.
12. *Yosemite Nature Notes* XXV:11 (November 1946), 126-129.
13. *Yosemite Nature Notes* XXVI:7 (July 1947), 83-84.
14. "Ta-bu-ce Howard," www.ancestry.com/.
15. Sargent, Pioneers in Petticoats, 14; *Yosemite Nature Notes* XXVI:7(July 1947), 85.
16. *Yosemite Nature Notes*, XXVI:7 (July 1947), 83-84.
17. *Mariposa Gazette*, October 29, 1931; Yosemite Nature Notes XXVI:7 (July 1947), 127-129.
18. *Yosemite Nature Notes* XXVI:7; "No Bread Lines for Yosemite Indians," www.thehive.modbee.

Louisa Strentzel Muir: A Founder's Mainstay
1. *Pasadena Star News* (Pasadena, CA), May 27, 1963; Harriet Burt, "Louie Strentzel Muir Through the Eyes of Her Daughter, Helen," http://martinez.patch.com/blog_posts/louie-strentzel-muir-through-the-eyes-of-her-daughter-helen/.
2. Patty and Steve Pauly, "Louie Strentzel Muir: A Biography," http://www.sierraclub.org/john_muir_exhibit/people/louie_muir_bio.aspx/.
3. Ibid.
4. Ibid.
5. *Oakland Tribune* (Oakland, CA), October 31, 1954.
6. Ibid.; John Muir, and William Bade, *The Life and Letters of John Muir* (Boston: Houghton Mifflin Company, 1924), Vol. 2, 114-118.
7. Muir and Bade, *Life and Letters*.

8. Donald Worster, *A Passion for Nature: The Life of John Muir* (Stockton, CA: University of the Pacific, 1997), 144-146; www.martinezhistory.org/ muir_history.HTM/.

9. Muir and Bade, *Life and Letters*.

10. Ibid.

11. Worster, *Passion for Nature*, 144.

12. *Independent Press Telegram*, January 15, 1975.

13. Worster, 161.

14. Louie Muir to John Muir, August 9, 1888, http://digitalcollections.pacific. edu/cdm/compoundobject/collection/muirletters/id/11323/rec/2/; Norman Risjord, *Representative Americans: Populists & Progressives* (Lanham, MD: Rowman & Littlefield Publishers, 2005), 228.

15. www.martinezhistory.org/muir_history.HTM/.

16. Ibid.

17. http://digitalcollections.pacific.edu/cdm/compoundobject/collection/ muirletters/id/10729/rec/1/.

18. Margaret Sanborn, *Yosemite: Its Discovery, Its Wonders, & Its People* (New York: Random House, 1981), 103.

19. Carl P. Russell, *One Hundred Years in Yosemite: The Story of a Great Park and Its Friends* (Berkeley: University of California Press, 1947), 133-134.

20. John Muir to Louie Muir, October 24, 1890, www.digitalcollections. pacific.edu/; Worster, 169-172.

21. www.martinezhistory.org/muir_history.HTM/.

22. Ibid.; Sally M. Miller and Daryl Morrison, *John Muir: Family, Friends & Adventure* (Albuquerque: University of New Mexico, 1983), 57.

23. Worster, 169; www.legendarylearningnow.com/johnmuir/.

24. Louie Muir to John Muir, June 21, 1893, www.digitalcollections.pacific. edu/.

25. www.martinezhistory.org/muir_history/.

26. Worster, *Passion for Nature*, 223-229.

27. *Pasadena Star News*.

28. Ibid.

Sarah Dutcher & Lady Jane Franklin: Adventurous Lady-Tourists

1. Margaret Sanborn, *Yosemite: Its Discovery, Its Wonders, & Its People* (New York: Random House, 1981), 153-154; Carl P. Russell, *One Hundred Years in Yosemite: The Story of a Great Park and Its Friends* (Berkeley: University of California Press, 1947), 79-80.

2. *The Defiance Democrat* (Defiance, OH), January 11, 1873; Nelson B. Keyes, *The Real Book About Our National Parks* (New York: Doubleday & Co., Inc., 1957), 36-39.

3. Julius Birge, *Awakening in the Desert* (Boston: Badger Books, 1912), 406-407.

4. Shirley Sargent, *Pioneers in Petticoats* (Los Angeles: Trans-Anglo Books Los Angeles, 1966), 44.

5. http://www.stanford.edu/galic/history/halfdome/dutcher_clark.html.

6. James Hutchings, *In the Heart of the Sierras* (Paris, France: Ulan Books, 1886), 215-219.

7. Ibid.

8. www.nps.gov/SallieDutcher/.

9. Ellen Berkovich, "Photog Carleton Watkins Blazed New Trails," *The New Mexican Magazine* Vol. 28 (March 31-April 6, 2000).

10. Peter E. Palmquist, *Carleton Watkins: Photographer of the North American West* (Albuquerque: University of New Mexico Press, 1983), 112-115.

11. www.stanford.edu/Dutcher/.

12. *Daily Alta California* (San Francisco), January 9, 1886.

13. Shirley Sargent, *Pioneers in Petticoats* (Los Angeles: Trans-Anglo Books Los Angeles, 1966), 45.

14. *Indiana Democrat* (Indiana, PA), August 5, 1875; *Perry Chief* (Perry, IA), July 31, 1875.

15. *Perry Chief.*

16. Ibid.

17. www.nls.uk/franklin/.

18. Ibid.; *The Argus* (Melbourne, Australia), February 19, 1932.

19. *Territorial Enterprise* (Virginia City, Nevada), September 20, 1861.

20. *Salt Lake Tribune*, November 23, 1890; *The Mercury* (CITY, STATE), July 22, 1875.

Florence Hutchings: A Rebel Lost Too Soon

1. *San Francisco Call*, September 26, 1899; *Sacramento Bee*, May 9, 1942; Shirley Sargent, *Pioneers in Petticoats* (Los Angeles: Trans-Anglo Books, 1966), 35-37.

2. Ibid.

3. Knave column, *Oakland Tribune*, March 15, 1964.

4. Ibid.; *San Francisco Call*, September 26, 1899; *Sacramento Bee*, May 9, 1942.

5. Ibid.

6. http://www.undiscovered-yosemite.com/florence-hutchings.html/.

7. Carl P. Russell, *One Hundred Years in Yosemite: The Story of a Great Park and Its Friends* (Berkeley: University of California Press, 1947), 97.

8. Ibid.

9. www.cdn.calisphere.org/muirletters.

10. Russell, 115.

11. Ibid.
12. Knave column; Nelson B. Keyes, *The Real Book About Our National Parks*, 86; Shirley Sargent, *Pioneers in Petticoats*, 35-38.
13. Shirley Sargent, *Yosemite & Its Innkeepers*, 11-13.
14. Ibid.; Russell, 100-101.
15. Knave column; www.undiscovered-yosemite.com/Florence-Hutchings/.
16. Sargent, *Pioneers in Petticoats*, 35-38.
17. Russell, 100-101.
18. *San Francisco Call*; *Sacramento Bee*.
19. Theresa Yelverston, *Zanita: A Tale of the Yosemite* (New York: Hurd & Houghton, 1872), 160-162.
20. Russell, 182.
21. Knave column; Sargent, *Pioneers in Petticoats*, 64.
22. www.nps.org/FlorenceHutchings/.
23. Ibid.
24. *San Francisco Call*; *Sacramento Bee*.
25. Ibid.

Clare Hodges: First Female Ranger in the Nation

1. John W. Bingaman, *Guardians of the Yosemite: A Story of the First Rangers* (Yosemite: Literary Licensing, Yosemite National Park Service, 1961), 97.
2. Nelson B. Keyes, *The Real Book About Our National Parks* (New York: Doubleday & Co., Inc., 1957)36-39.
3. Polly W. Kaufman, "Pioneer Women Naturalist in the Park Service," *Forest & Conservation History*, January 1990; *Them Were the Days Magazine*, Fall 1996.
4. Laurence Degnan, "The Yosemite Valley School," *Yosemite Nature Notes*, XXXV:2 (February 1956), 15-19.
5. *Pacific Short Story Club Magazine*, Vol. 7-10 (1914).
6. http://www.cca.edu/news/2012/08/22/julia-florence-parker-textiles-master-tradition-spring-2006/; *Lowell Sun* (Lowell, MA), August 20, 1918.
7. Department of Interior Hiring Card, May 22, 1918; *Sunset*.
8. *Sunset*; *Fresno Bee*.
9. Robert W. Young, "Ladies Who Wear the Uniforms of the National Park Service," *Planning & Civil Comment*, 28:1 (March 1962).
10. Hiring card.
11. www.ancestry.com/.
12. Degnan, "Yosemite Valley School," 15-19; *Lima News* (Lima. OH), June 1, 1919.
13. www.ancestry.com/.
14. *Fresno Bee*.

15. *Lima News.*
16. *Pacific Short Story Club Magazine,* Vol. 1-3, 1914.
17. www.ancestry.com/; Bingaman, *Guardians,* 97.

Erin Davenport: Archaeologist and Basket Weaver
1. *Atchison Daily Globe* (Atchison, KS), September 15, 1974.
2. Quotations from Erin Davenport are from author interviews: via e-mail on October 23, 2012, and November 26, 2012, and by phone on October 25, 2012.
3. Shirley Sargent, *Pioneers in Petticoats* (Los Angeles: Trans-Anglo Books, 1966), 14.
4. *Washington Post,* October 10, 1909.
5. Elizabeth Godfrey, *Yosemite Indians* (Yosemite: Yosemite Natural History Association, 1973), 18-19; www.californiabaskets.com/.
6. Molly Mitchell, "Julia Florence Parker, Textiles Master of Tradition, Spring 2006," http://www.cca.edu/news/2012/08/22/julia-florence-parker-textiles-master-tradition-spring-2006/.

Index

About the Author

Chris Enss is an author, scriptwriter and comedienne who has written for television and film, and performed on cruise ships and on stage. She has worked with award-winning musicians, writers, directors, producers, and as a screenwriter for Tricor Entertainment, but her passion is for telling the stories of the men and women who shaped the history and mythology of the American West. Some of the most famous names in history, not to mention film and popular culture, populate her books. She revealed the stories behind the many romances of William "Buffalo Bill" Cody, who moved on from his career as a scout on the plains to take the enormously successful performance spectacle of Buffalo Bill's Wild West to audiences throughout the United States and Europe between 1883 and 1916. And she told the stories of the many talented and daring women who performed alongside men in the Wild West shows, and who changed the way the world thought about women forever through the demonstration of their skills. Chris has brought her sensitive eye and respect for their work to the stories of more contemporary American entertainers, as well. Her books reveal the lives of John Wayne, Roy Rogers, and Dale Evans, bringing to light stories gleaned from family interviews and archives. The most famous American couple of the 19th century, General George Armstrong Custer and Elizabeth Bacon Custer, drew her scrutiny as well. *None Wounded, None Missing, All Dead* reveals the personality of the fiery, lively Libbie and her lifelong effort to burnish her husband's reputation. Chris took readers along the trail with the Intrepid Posse as their horses thundered after the murderer of Dodge City dance hall favorite Dora Hand, and she turned her attention to the famous Sam Sixkiller, legendary Cherokee sheriff, but perhaps most extraordinary are the stories of the ordinary men and women who shaped American history when they came west as schoolmarms, gold miners, businessmen, madams, and mail-order brides.